WALKS ON THE
WEST PENNINE MOORS

A COMPANION GUIDE TO THE
RECREATION AREA

by GLADYS SELLERS

Illustrations by R. B. Evans

D1395790

©Gladys Sellers 1978

SNB 902363 20 4

First published 1979
Revised Edition 1983

Cover: Winter Hill and Rivington Pike from Pike Stones

Published by Cicerone Press
Harmony Hall, Milnthorpe, Cumbria LA7 7QE.

CONTENTS

ACKNOWLEDGEMENTS

I should like to thank the following friends for placing their local knowledge at my disposal: Miss A. Palmer, Mr. & Mrs. J. W. Rostron, Mr. W. Sherborne, and Mr. P. L. Walkden.

The responsibility for the selection and description of the walks, is, however, mine alone. In addition I should like to thank Mr. J. Heyes, Deputy Librarian of the Chorley and District Library for his assistance with my searches for information.

Gladys Sellers, 1978

The Coke Ovens, Broadhead Valley,
(Walk no. 2.6)

Part One

THE WEST PENNINE MOORS RECREATION AREA

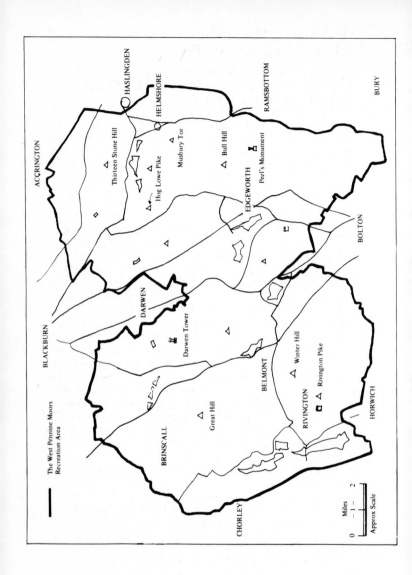

The West Pennine Moors
Recreation Area

ACCRINGTON

HASLINGDEN

HELMSHORE

RAMSBOTTOM

BURY

Thirteen Stone Hill

Hog Lowe Pike

Musbury Tor

Bull Hill

EDGEWORTH

Peel's Monument

BLACKBURN

DARWEN

Darwen Tower

Winter Hill

Rivington Pike

BELMONT

RIVINGTON

BOLTON

HORWICH

BRINSCALL

Great Hill

CHORLEY

Miles

0 — 1 — 2

Approx Scale

6

INTRODUCING THE
WEST PENNINE MOORS

People who live in the immediate vicinity have walked these moors for pleasure for the last 50 years or more, sometimes risking trespass in so doing. Attitudes gradually change, and recently the need for local recreation areas has been accepted. The Water Act of 1973 was an important factor, for it united in a single regional authority the many smaller urban water boards that then existed in the district, and at the same time obliged them to consider possible recreational uses of their land and water. Recognising the importance of Anglezarke, as their chosen area was then called, the Lancashire County Council carried out studies and surveys leading to the publication of a Consultative Report in 1973. After the reorganisation of local government in 1974, the responsibility for developing — or conserving — Anglezarke was divided amongst the two county authorities of Lancashire and Greater Manchester, the borough councils of Blackburn, Chorley, Hyndburn, and Rossendale, and the metropolitan borough councils of Bolton and Bury. They, together with the North West Water Authority, jointly decided to prepare a comprehensive recreational plan. Further surveys and studies were carried out and published, but before preparing a plan of action, they held a number of consultative meetings all around the district to discover what local people thought of their ideas. These meetings were extremely well attended, and some of the ideas the experts put forward were not too well received. People were concerned that their locality should be conserved rather than developed. In particular, the County's original name for the area, Anglezarke, was widely objected to, and the present rather cumbersome title of West Pennine Moors Recreation Area was adopted. In this book it will be abbreviated to Area, and whenever the word is used with a capital A, that is its meaning.

Early in 1978 the Lancashire County Council, on behalf of all the bodies named above, produced its report, "Approach to a Plan". This report puts forward the view that in this day and age of the motor car and leisure, the Area will suffer more from the problems of an influx of visitors without a plan than with one. Its Plan aims to give effective management of recreational activities and the traffic they generate, and to conserve and enhance the Area. Any measures introduced to further these aims will be designed so as not to interfere with the farming, forestry, and water catchment, and living conditions in the

7

Area. A difficult requirement indeed! After due regard for the outcome of the public participation meetings held in March and April, the County will produce its Draft Plan. There is the possibility of a Public Enquiry, and then the Final Structure Plan can be approved.

The Area covers 90 square miles and its boundaries are roughly as follows: Starting arbitrarily at Horwich, the boundary follows the M61 from a point about 1 mile west of that town to Chorley, where it follows the A674 to Feniscowles. There it turns east along a minor road to Darwen, omits the Darwen urban area, skirts the south of Accrington, and then turns south-east to follow the line of the old railway through Haslingden almost to Ramsbottom, where it turns west a little and follows the B6214 down through Tottington to the B6196 at Ainsworth. From here it takes a devious course round the northern urban fringe of Bolton, excludes Horwich, and finally turns sharply south-west down the B5238 to the M61.

The ground enclosed by the boundaries is predominantly high moorland divided by broad valleys and steep-sided wooded cloughs, many of which contain the reservoirs of the North West Water Authority. This combination of lake, wood, and moor produces scenery that is particularly fine in the western part, and gives some of the best walks, not only in terms of scenery, but of the interesting things to be seen. The widely differing habitats provided by moorlands, streams, and reservoirs means that the Area supports a surprisingly wide range of plants and birds, and the Nature Conservancy Council has designated the Area as a "Conservation Zone" of county-wide importance.

There is a long history of man's settlement in the Area, not only in the valleys but on the moors themselves. There are a number of interesting remains, ranging from pre-historic monuments to early industrial settlements. On the debit side of man's usage is the large number of mineral workings scattered throughout the Area. Their decline has resulted in some useful terrain for recreation — for example, rock climbing in many of the quarries — but there is much derelict and unsightly ground.

The state of play in 1982

In 1980 the County Council produced its Draft Local Plan and this now awaits approval by the Secretary of State for the Environment. A few of its measures have been implemented, mainly better car parking with toilets at Anglezarke and Jumbles Reservoirs. The North West Water Authority has started some afforestation above Lead Mine Valley and this has meant major changes to one or two walks.

1. ROCKS, MINERALS AND MINING

A large number of the rocks of Northern England were formed by material deposited by the Great Upper Carboniferous Delta. This was part of the geological drainage system that operated in the Northern Hemisphere — for England did not yet exist — some 300 million years ago. It follows that the rocks were all laid down by waterborne particles, that is to say, sand and silt, and have been solidified into rock in the aeons of time that have passed since then. These rocks are broadly classified into Millstone grit, Lower, Upper and Middle Coal Measures. The Coal Measures themselves are a complex sequence of related strata which are repeated several times. These have been classified as fossiliferous shale, barren shale, and mudstone, sandy shale, sandstone, and coal.

Today, after faulting and tilting brought about by earth movements, these rocks are no longer as they were laid down. By means of the fossils present, it has been shown that the rocks of Lester Mill Quarry, Anglezarke, for example, belong to the same strata as some of those that can be seen by the River Roddlesworth at Tockholes, and that they are not the same as those in Healey Nab Quarry, which is very much nearer. The strata have mostly been classified, identified, and named, so that we can refer to the Fletcher Bank grit of Lester Mill Quarry, the Rough Rock of Healey Nab, or the Holcombe Brook coal seam at Rivington. Technically speaking, most of the rock referred to in common speech as 'gritstone' is a modified sandstone.

The glaciers or their melt water streams of the last glacial epoque some 8-9 thousand years ago produced the valley in which the Anglezarke and Rivington Reservoirs were built and the other broad valleys that separate the high moorland blocks of the Area. These valleys have since been modified by the action of the rivers themselves. As the glaciers retreated they left a thick layer of boulder clay on the lower ground, whilst the higher ground, standing above the level of the ice, did not collect this layer.

Having established the geological groundwork, let us consider a little of the detail seen as you walk in the Area. Much of the quarrying and mining that went on, say, a century ago, has ceased. Some deposits such as the coal have been worked out, others have become uneconomic to work, and the Area has a vast legacy of unsightly remains. They do, however, lay bare the bones of the earth to the enquiring mind.

The useful properties of the various layers of sandstone vary considerably. Some contain more coarse particles and are harder than those that contain more of the fine mud and silt particles. These split easily and in times past have been used for paving stones. Quarries tended to work a stone for a particular purpose: at Lester Mill Quarry the stone was mainly for road sets and kerbstones, whilst in the Rossendale valley the Haslingden Flags were used for pavements and roofing stone. One especially pure white gritstone called ganister has been used to line blast furnaces, and fragments can be found in many places round Anglezarke.

Lead and barytes are two other minerals that occur in the Area. Lead was worked in earlier times in three places on Anglezarke moor where there has been faulting and fracturing in the Fletcher Bank Grits. The most important place is in Limestone Clough, locally called Lead Mine Valley, where lead occurs as galena and is accompanied by barytes, witherite, iron pyrites, and some calcite. The vein was at a depth of about 43 yards and was 6-36 inches wide. Mining was carried on here as early as the 17th century and continued up to the mid 18th century when the vein was exhausted. Another vein that was worked is just below Drinkwater Farm on Gt. Hill. At neither place can fragments of galena often be found today — they've all been picked up, but the heavy white barytes (barium sulphate) is still quite plentiful, and in places, so too is witherite: barium carbonate is a relatively rare mineral. Witherite is also very heavy, but is translucent and rather fibrous in appearance.

No less important than the quarrying of stone has been coal mining, now no longer carried out. A small privately owned colliery at Montcliffe, Horwich, was worked up to 1968 though mainly for fireclay. All workable seams are now exhausted. The most important seams are known as the Upper and Lower Mountain seams — indicative of where they were first mined — which was on Darwen and Winter Hills, although the seams cover a much more extensive area. These seams vary in thickness from 2-4 ft., and may be found at no great depth, particularly the Upper Mountain Seam. The Lower Mountain Seam outcrops in Stepback Brook, Tockholes, and near the top of the adjacent Cartridge Hill, and was mined there in the middle of the 19th century. Another seam known as the Holcombe Brook seam outcrops near the Belmont-Rivington road, and at one time was mined to supply Rivington Hall with coal. Today nothing can be seen of these workings, indeed, it is hard to find even fragments of coal, though sizeable pieces can be found around some of the old shafts on Darwen Hill and Moor.

In many places the coal is underlaid by fireclay and this was worked on Smithills and Wilders Moor to make stoneware, and again near Hoddlesden for making glazed bricks. Today the mudstone deposits near Withnell are used for making an engineering brick, and clay at Horwich is used for tile making. Sand deposited by the retreating glaciers' melt water is worked on the fringe of the Area near Chorley. The most recent deposit of all, peat, has been worked near Whittlestone Head, Darwen, for horticultural purposes.

2. MOORLAND PLANTS

Most people think that only grass and heather grow on the moors, or, if they think a bit longer, will add rushes and bilberries to the list. In fact, there's a lot more than that, and it is useful to know a little about them when you are out walking. There's no need to bother with Latin names or anything like that!

If you've done a few of these walks you will probably have noticed that you don't usually get your feet wet when you're going through heather. Everybody knows what heather is like, especially when it's in flower in August, but there is a similar plant called crowberry. This grows in the same sort of dry places as the heather and looks rather like it except that it has much longer spiky leaves and it has little black berries in late summer. They are not poisonous, but it's no pleasure to eat them. Now crowberry, which you can recognise by its bright green mat at all times of the year gives delightful springy walking, quite different from heather, which is often hard work. Bilberry is another plant that likes the same sort of drier place. Bracken likes it drier still. You'll never get your feet wet in a bracken patch!

Having spoken of the plants of the drier places, let us consider those of the wet ones. The really wet ones grow cotton grass, easily recognised by its tuft of 'cotton' just after it's flowered in June. Anywhere you see thick with cotton grass is best avoided unless you're wearing wellies. Another plant of the wet places is purple moor grass: that tall grass that grows into big tussocks. It gives truly abominable walking especially in July and August when its long flower stalks — grasses have flowers, ask any hay fever sufferer — hide the tussocks. There's just one other sort of grass that you might mistake for purple moor grass. It makes smaller tussocks and its leaves are wiry, not flat, and it still likes the wet places. It's called wavy hair grass, and it's probably the commonest grass on the moors. There's another tuft forming plant called Mat grass after the mat of decaying yellow leaves that form at its base. It prefers the drier pastures, poor ones at that, and doesn't offer much nourishment for sheep. Otherwise most of the grass isn't grass at all, but sedges and rushes.

Sedges don't only grow round the edges of ponds and lakes: quite a lot of the plants of the wet places in the moors are also sedges. If they're in flower, it is easy to distinguish a sedge from a grass but if not you need to look carefully. The sedges have two quite distinct types of flower on the same stalk, one above the other, and these stalks have a triangular cross section and they're solid, whereas the flower stalks on grasses are round and hollow. If they're not in flower, look at the leaves. Sedge leaves have a very prominent mid rib giving them a cross-section like a flattened triangle, and a lot of them spread their leaves from a central point in a triangular shape. The difficulties only start if you want to put a name to any particular sedge — the sedges named in this book are probably right, but it's possible they are not!

This may prompt you to wonder what is the difference between a rush and a sedge. Rushes all have round solid stems, and as grasses are round and hollow and sedges triangular and solid there's no real problem. There's more than one sort of rush, though, but the common one all over the moors is the heath rush. It grows spread about like grass, 6-8 inches (15-20 cms) high, it has stiff wiry leaves and the 'flower' is a couple of knobbly brown things that last on the plant all winter.

I fear you may be more interested in hearing about pretty and exciting flowers, and want to know why we do not have any on the moors. It's largely because of the nature of the underlying rocks. All wild plants derive their nourishment from the weathering of the rocks which produce the soil and minerals to feed them. The gritstones and shales of our moorland do not produce much mineral matter. In addition the high rainfall, 50-60 inches (125-150 cms), per annum washes away that which is available almost as it is made. These two factors combine to encourage the production of peat which in turn produces land too acidic to allow the growth of a wide range of plants. A few plants like rhododendron and heather thrive on an acid soil, most others prefer a neutral or limey soil. It so happens that most of our lovely wild flowers like a limey soil, and we haven't got one in this area. That's why there's so few harebells in our hedegrows and why we have the white bedstraw instead of the yellow bedstraw that grows around Malham. There are just a few places in the Area where some lovely wildflowers can be found, but until the general public are happy to see these flowers where they grow and not to pick them by the wilting handful, then these places must remain known only to the naturalists.

3. PRE-HISTORY OF THE MOORS

The archaeological remains in the Area are probably more numerous than one would think: at the same time they are probably smaller and less interesting than one would have hoped. This part of England never had the wealth of archaeological remains that exist in the south of England, and of those there are, many have been damaged or even destroyed. Our small remains are best appreciated with some knowledge of the general pattern of pre-history, defined as anything that happened before writing was in use. In Great Britain this art was brought over by the Romans, so pre-history starts with the very earliest man, possibly 500,000 B.C., and ends at about 50 A.D.

It must be made clear at the beginning that dates used in pre-history are necessarily very vague. Not only is there the difficulty in putting a date to any place or object (and the older the greater the problem) but in addition, when talking about the end of the New Stone Age and the start of the Bronze Age, for example, this does not mean that it was clean cut and sharp. It simply means that fewer stone axes and scrapers were used as they were gradually replaced by bronze ones. Furthermore, ideas travelled very slowly and as new cultures generally came from the continent to the south of England, changes are likely to have taken place there possibly centuries before the same changes took place in the north of England.

The very earliest men, the Old Stone Age men, were hunters and collectors of berries and herbs. They lived in caves and used massive stone hand axes, that is to say, a shaped and sharpened stone held in the hand. None of their remains have been found in the Area. The oldest remains in the Area are the microliths made by Mesolithic Man or Middle Stone Age Man, dated variously 8000-12,000 B.C. These microliths have been found on **Bull Hill** and other places, though on Bull Hill there have been so many that a chipping floor or workshop is thought to have been sited there. Though very small, roughly the size of a finger nail, technically they are a great advance on a hand axe as they were made to set in a bone or wooden handle which has long since disappeared. These people were hunters and food collectors like their ancestors.

By about 3,500 B.C. agriculture, discovered in the Middle East as early as 10,000 B.C. had arrived in southern Britain, and the farmers of the New Stone Age became established. Many remains have been found there such as long barrows, cause-

14

Pike Stones

ways, pottery and bones, but so far, nothing in our Area. Not until we come to Megalithic Man some 1000 years later do we find any such remains, when we have **Pike Stones**, the oldest man made object of any size in the Area. It is thought to have been built between 2700 and 1000 B.C. Pike Stones is the remains of a five slab burial chamber and stands on a low egg shaped mound of packed stones 160 ft long and 60 ft wide. Originally the chambered tomb would have been earth covered. The outline can be quite easily seen except in summer when the long grass veils it. At the wider end this ring of packed stones curves round like a pair of horns to make a forecourt where ritual could have been carried out in front of the entrance. Megalithic Man made many much bigger and more elaborate chambered tombs now called Dolmens or Cromlechs. He also erected standing stones and stone circles and started to build the first Stonehenge, which was later added to by the Bronze Age people. Possibly he erected the stone circle on **Thirteen Stone Hill**, but so little is left it is difficult to be sure. The stone circles on **Chetham Close** are thought to be the remains of Neolithic or Bronze Age burial mounds.

The New Stone Age very gradually merged into the Early Bronze Age for which a nominal date of 1600 B.C. has been given. The early, middle and late bronze ages lasted 1,000

Round Loaf, with Great Hill behind.

years and were ultimately replaced by the Iron Age in around 500 B.C. This period of 1,000 years has left quite a number of characteristic tumuli or round barrows in the Area. The word 'barrow' may be derived from the Anglo-Saxon word 'beorg'. In addition 'lowe' is a Saxon word for burial mound, and there are quite a number of Lowes in the Area, for example, **Slipper Lowe** at Tockholes, **Hog Lowe Pike** above the Broadhead valley, and **The Lowe** at White Coppice. Around this time there was a marked improvement in climate. It became drier and warmer. Evidence for this has been obtained from examination of pollen obtained from the deepest layers of peat. Every sort of pollen grain is quite characteristic of the plant that produces it, and it can be recognised under the microscope. Very fortunately the outer skin of pollen grains is an exceedingly tough and durable material and pre-historic pollen grains have survived at the bottom of the peat layer on the moor. These grains belong to birches, alders, and oaks which won't grow on the moors in today's climate. Their position gives additional confirmation, for peat only forms in a cold wet climate, and then at the rate of about 5 cms per 100 years, which enables a rough date to be put on these tumuli like **Round Loaf, Noon Hill,** and at **Quarlton**. It is quite clear that the better climate enabled the bronze age men to live, die and be buried on the moors, for practically the only remains of them is in the burial mounds. Very few bronze age tools have been found compared with the number of flint tools. The latter became blunt very rapidly and were no doubt then discarded. Bronze was a valuable substance that could be re-melted, and though bronze tools may have been lost, it is unlikely that they were ever thrown away. When Noon Hill was excavated in the 1950s there was evidence of four burials. Scrapers, arrow heads and an urn were found. These are now housed in Bolton Municipal Museum.

Pottery in particular enables dates to be assigned rather more accurately and 1400 B.C. has been suggested for this tumulus, whilst the nearby one on **Winter Hill** is thought to be older. Very little can be seen today of either of these mounds. Excavation is a destructive process. Round Loaf has not been excavated but on general shape is thought to be of the same age. A mound in the grounds of **White Hall**, Over Darwen, was excavated late last century, and evidence of ten bronze age burials was found. Three pottery urns have been restored and are displayed in the Reference Library at Darwen.

One way of dating a find of any sort is to compare it and the place where it was found with other finds and sites about which more is known. Pottery is very useful because it is reasonably durable even though early pieces were not so well fired as present day pottery. Its shape and above all its decoration help to date it. There were fashions even then. Radio carbon dating is of limited value in dating these early finds. A substantial amount of carbonaceous material is needed for the test, and so often there isn't enough, or any at all.

Around 500 B.C. settlers from Europe using superior iron tools and weapons invaded this country. They speedily overran the existing population and thus the Celtic Iron Age was established. At the same time the climate changed and became colder and wetter, and the Iron Age men were the first to wear trousers. Villages and field patterns developed as agriculture became established as the way of life rather than hunting — not that they were peaceable people, far from it, for their chief remain is the hill fort. Again this was most highly developed in the south of England, and Maiden Castle is the best example. In our Area, the top of **Twa Lads Moor**, Horwich, is thought to have been crowned by an Iron Age fort, and flanked by ditches, but precious little remains to be seen today. The Druidic culture dates from this period. Little is known of the religion of these people who were driven westwards into Wales by the Romans, and today's Druidic rites are largely the invention of the romantic minds of the mid 18th century. What little evidence there is suggests that the Druids formed a body of essential knowledge such as the working of the calendar, medicine, religious practices and poetry.

As the Romans gradually subdued the country after their successful invasion, they brought with them the new skill of writing. Pre-history in England was coming to an end. The Romans built a network of roads to connect the forts they built to subdue the country. In Lancashire the best known fort was at

Ribchester and it was connected to the one at Manchester by Watling Street, which runs through the Area from Starling near Bury through Affetside, Edgworth, and Grimehills to the outskirts of Blackburn. Today there is nothing to be seen of the road above ground. Excavations in the 1950s near **Bottom o' Knotts Brow**, Turton, revealed a portion of road. More recent excavations near **Pallet Farm**, Edgworth, laid bare another portion. Both these excavations were filled in again. The bridge across the stream below the **Crown and Thistle Inn**, Grimehills, is reputedly of Roman origin. There have been finds of coins in various places, but regretfully, there is virtually nothing else left.

4. ANCIENT MONUMENTS AND MUSEUMS

There are eleven scheduled Ancient Monuments including three museums that are protected by the 1913-1953 Acts. These Ancient Monuments comprise the three museums, five pre-historic burial mounds, two headless crosses and a portion of Roman road. Except the museums, which are very fine buildings indeed, none of the Ancient Monuments are very impressive and not all are worth a special visit. The policy of the Department of the Environment is to schedule a site even if it has been excavated and covered in again. This goes some way to ensure that it is protected against destruction or damage, and this is the case as far as the Roman road at the Bottom o' Knotts Brow, Turton is concerned. It was excavated in the 1950s, established as genuine, and filled in again. Similarly, at the tumulus on Winter Hill, little can be seen today.

The burial mounds are all remote from any road and are visited on the following walks:

Round Loaf, Anglezarke,	Walk No. 7, Section 1
Pike Stones, Anglezarke,	Walk No. 7, Section 1
Noon Hill Ring Cairn, Winter Hill,	Walk No. 1 & 5, Section 1
Round Barrow on Winter Hill,	Walk No. 1 & 5, Section 1
Stone Circles on Chetham Close,	Walk No. 5, Section 2

Some notes about them are at the end of the relevant walk. In addition there is more information about them in the previous chapter on the pre-history of the moors.

The **Headless Cross** at Anderton is by the roadside at a cross roads on a minor road behind the Millstone Hotel, Horwich, which is at the northern end of the reservoir embankment on the A673. Tradition says that the figure on it is St. Anthony. When so many crosses lost their heads during the reign of Henry VIII and Edward VI the pillars were sometimes put to other uses. In due time this one became a sign post pointing the way to Blegburn, (note the spelling), Bolton, Wigan, and Preston. Fairly obviously the lettering is not nearly as old as the rest of the cross. During the building of the Anglezarke and Rivington Reservoirs, the cross was removed from its traditional place and eventually found its way to Viscount Leverhulme's Bungalow Gardens. The Lancashire County Council restored it to its present position in 1945. The two-position stocks were there at that time.

Affetside – Headless Cross

The **Headless Cross** at Affetside stands by the road in the village, the approximate site of the Roman road, Watling Street. It is, at the moment, the only one of these Ancient Monuments bearing the plate of H.M. Office of Works indicating that it is an Ancient Monument. The Lancashire and Cheshire Antiquarian Society investigated it in the early years of this century. They considered it to be the remains of a Market Cross, possibly from Jacobean times, indicating a nearby field where a market was held.

The three museums, Smithills Hall, Turton Tower, and Higher Mill are all quite different from each other both as far as the buildings themselves are concerned and their displays. Higher Mill is unique, being devoted to early cotton manufacturing processes. Hall i' th' Wood is another museum only just outside the Area, and having strong associations with the Industrial Revolution, is worth a visit before visiting Higher Mill Museum.

SMITHILLS HALL, BOLTON

Lies just off the B6207 where that road crosses the Moss Bank Way ring road, the A58. It is well sign posted. A bus runs direct to the Hall from Bolton town centre. The hall is a large complex structure of various periods, much of it in black and white

Smithills Hall

work, but only a relatively small part, the oldest, is open to the public. The oldest of all, the Great Hall, is all that remains of a manor house thought to be older than 1350, and one of the oldest in Lancashire. It has been carefully restored and sparsely furnished in the style of the times. Much more ornate, and in great contrast to the austerity of the Great Hall, is the East Wing, added in Henry VIII's reign. This is a truly beautiful room, whose walls are lined with fine linen-fold panelling. It is appropriately furnished and gives a picture of gracious living. Of considerable local interest are the pictures of old Bolton lining the main corridors.

A little distance away is the old coach house and stables, now used as a restaurant. They are Grade 2 listed buildings. The whole of the buildings are surrounded by fine lawns and gardens backed by woodland, where there is a nature trail. Even better in wet weather is a nature trail cabin, where a series of photographs, diagrams, pressed leaves and grasses, mounted birds, insects and mammals show all the things that might be seen on the trail, together with a geologically based explanation. The whole is extremely well done, and a whole afternoon can be spent there.

TURTON TOWER, BOLTON

Turton Tower is of a rather different character from Smithills and is a Grade 1 listed building. It lies just off the B6391 a few hundred yards south of Chapeltown, is signposted and there is a bus stop at the door. Parking is within the grounds of the Tower itself. You usually drive right up to the Tower, feeling

21

very grand, before turning right into the car park.

The Tower is quite an impressive structure dating from 1400 A.D. It is built around an ancient 'pele tower', a type of fortified house fairly common in the North of England and usually built as a means of defence against the raiding Scots in the time of Robert the Bruce. Later on the fine looking black and white farmhouse was added by the Orrell family, and in 1596 a William Orrell raised the height of the tower in order to increase the height of the rooms in it. This can be seen quite clearly. Humphrey Chetham, of Chetham's Hospital fame, is the Tower's most famous owner. It changed hands a number of times after his ownership and was finally given to the Turton U.D.C. by the widow of Sir Lees Knowles in 1930. Today it is cared for by the Borough of Blackburn.

Entry costs a few pence. Inside there are some fine pieces of carved oak furniture, some of them from Bradshaw Hall, now demolished. The conference room is pleasant, but somehow too modern to be in keeping with a pele tower. Only this room and the dining room seem to be as they were, rooms for living in, as opposed to rooms for displaying collections of furniture or other articles. The top room of the tower is in this latter category although it really looks the part of a fortified house. It has bare stone walls, a collection of swords and suits of armour on the walls, stags heads and hunting horns. This first impression of character is unfortunately spoiled by the ceiling, obviously modern and quite out of keeping with the rest of the room. The Tower was re-roofed about five years ago and no heed seems to have been paid to doing the job in harmony with the rest of the building.

Outside there is a water wheel, brought from Turton Bottoms. It is intended to restore this and to install it as a working specimen.

Despite these criticisms of the place, it is still well worth a visit.

Higher Hill Museum

HIGHER MILL MUSEUM, HELMSHORE

This is a museum with a difference. There's none other even remotely like it in the Area, nor even in the whole of Lancashire. It is a late eighteenth century fulling mill in working order — incredible! (Fulling is the final processing given to woollen cloth such as is used for blankets.) The mill lies on the B6235 road which links the B6232 and the B6215 roads on the south-west side of Haslingden. It has a sign-post at the entrance and is not hard to find, though its closeness to another old mill is at first puzzling. Just drive in.

The building itself, recently renovated, makes two sides of a courtyard, and dating from 1789, looks very fine indeed. The ground floor is open Monday to Friday, 2.0 pm to 5.0 pm.

Admission costs 25p. This is the original part of the fulling mill and contains fulling machinery made in the early years of the nineteenth century and was worked by a water wheel right up to 1954. The water wheel has been restored and the banks of the reservoir strengthened, so the wheel can be worked for visitors. It is not, however, geared up to the machinery as it used to be, and some of that is demonstrated for you by means of an electric motor.

Upstairs there is a collection of cotton spinning machinery, including early examples of Arkwright's water frame and Hargreaves' spinning jenny. These are all in working order and are demonstrated to parties who have booked a tour. Unfortunately the dangers from primitive shafts and belts to people are such that this machinery can only be demonstrated to people on a guided tour. This must be pre-booked, and costs, at present, £3, or £5 at weekends and evenings. Parties must not exceed 20 people. Ring the Curator (Rossendale 26459) for an appointment.

The potential of this building, not just the museum of exhibits, but as a demonstration of cotton manufacture as it used to be carried out, is extremely high. If you or your family have ever been in the cotton industry, you'll find it particularly fascinating.*

HALL I' TH' WOOD, BOLTON
Lies off the A58 ring road between the A575 and the A676. It can just be seen a few hundred yards away on the north side of the ring road and is approached through a housing estate from it. It is sign posted, but not quite so well as Smithills Hall.

Hall i' th' Wood is yet another of Viscount Leverhulme's benefactions. He bought it in 1897 whilst he was still Mr Lever and gave it to Bolton Corporation together with sufficient money for its restoration, for it was then in very bad condition. The Hall's main claim to fame is that it is the place where Samuel Crompton was living when he invented the spinning mule in 1779; one of the most important inventions of the Industrial Revolution. Not that Crompton was one of the aristocracy, far from it. He was just one of a family of weavers who occupied the building with other families and farmers. As is fitting in such a building, much of its furniture is of a homely

---

* Remains of the cotton industry abound in the Area (see next chapter). Examples of machinery are displayed at the Textile Machinery Museum, Tonge Moor Library, Tonge Moor Road, Bolton.

Hall I'th' Wood

nature. There is a huge fireplace with an equally huge spit turned by an ingenious arrangement of stone weights, cheese presses, clothes presses, coffee mills turned by hand, goffer irons and, all manner of long forgotten domestic items. One room is devoted to Crompton's possessions and things connected with him. There is a spinning wheel he used as a child, a violin and an organ he made, pictures of his parents, his letters seeking financial backing for his invention, but rather disappointingly, only a small model of the mule itself. As a contrast to the grandeur of nearby Smithills Hall, it's very well worth a visit at the same time.

5. CONSERVATION AREAS

Conservation Areas do much to enhance the character of any particular region. In the years before cheap transport and universally available building materials made architectural styles deadly uniform, local geological structures limited the materials available and climate defined the style. Few houses and factories were built in other than this manner and thus architectural character was established. Every generation decries the efforts of its immediate predecessors as old fashioned and worthless, and so demolition has been the order of the day. However, over the last ten years public opinion has changed from this view to one that seeks to find and preserve the best examples that are left. Thus has come into being the concepts of the Conservation Area and the listed building. These ideas have been given legal backing by the Country Amenities Act of 1974 which requires local authorities to designate Conservation Areas and to take steps to preserve and enhance their character. A listed building is one of architectural or historic interest, and again is subject to the control of the local authority. These buildings include every type — farms, houses, mills, pubs, churches and monuments, and are graded by their quality. The standards for a Grade 1 building are very high, and there are only four of them within the Area. They are Smithills Hall, Rivington Hall Barn, Great House Barn, and Turton Tower. Grade 2 and 3 buildings are too numerous to list, but some outstanding ones are mentioned in the text of this book. Where many of these listed buildings occur together, that little area has a character all of its own, and it is areas like these that have been designated Conservation Areas. Some of these areas include considerable tracts of countryside such as at Wallsuches. There are no notice boards to indicate the areas, nor any boundary marks. The observer must have a map and an appreciative eye.

Most of the Conservation Areas are either close to starting points of walks or are passed through during the course of a walk. Few are worth a special visit unless you are especially interested in local architecture and conservation. Here are a few notes about them in alphabetical order.

ABBEY VILLAGE, CHORLEY, was built around and was totally dependant on a weaving mill, and even as late as December 30th, 1971, the last day the mill ran, there was no other employment in the village. It was built during the hey-day of the Industrial Revolution in 1846, and the original mill cottages that line Bolton Road make a fine avenue. Many are being modernised and the mill has found new uses. The village stands on the Bolton-Preston road, the A675, and can be usefully visited before Walk No. 4, Section 4.

AINSWORTH, RADCLIFFE, is a village with a degree of isolation and has retained its identity. The main road used to run in front of the pub, the Duke William. In those days it was an old coaching inn, still with its high doorway that would admit a coach to the rear. Close at hand is the Unitarian Chapel built in 1715 and enlarged and rebuilt through the years, but full of character. Its graveyard has possibly the best collection of old gravestones, many prior to 1800, in the Area. The Parish Church is not especially noteworthy, being largely rebuilt in early Victorian times, but just inside its lichgate is a pair of stumps that were once part of the village stocks. There are several rows of cottages still in good repair that keep the old village character intact. As the starting point of a good short walk, No. 8, Section 2, it is well worth a dual-purpose visit. The village stands on the B6196, Bury to Bradshaw road.

BARROW BRIDGE, BOLTON, is the site of one of the early 'model villages' of industrial Lancashire. It was founded in 1846 by Thomas Bazley, and the two spinning mills, long since demolished, employed 800 people. They were housed in the model village of which the curiously named Second, Third, Fourth, and Fifth Streets remain. These lie on Bazley Road up the hill from the bus stop. The school, Mechanics Institute, and a number of other old houses lie on it. Quite a number of these as well as the fine old houses in Barrow Bridge Road are Grade 2 listed buildings. Reverting to a bit more history, the mill changed hands and in 1876 the new owner died. The mills closed and the inhabitants had to seek work elsewhere. In the closing years of this century Barrow Bridge became a deserted village. Now the wheel of fortune has changed. Old mill cottages have become much sought after homes for all sorts of people. Still writing of mills, the prominent chimney at the junction of Moss Lane is listed as a Grade 2 building. One would hardly say that it's beautiful, but there are not many of them left, and chimneys are a very essential part of the Lancashire scene. Barrow Bridge is the starting point for Walk No. 10, Section 2, and is best approached from the Moss Bank Way ring road, Bolton, A58, bearing left all the time from Moss Bank Park traffic lights.

CHAPELTOWN, BOLTON, is only about ½ mile from Turton Bottoms and Edgworth and they can quite easily be visited together. The whole of the village street is attractive, but the finest part lies at the northern end. The pub, the Chetham Arms, is a grade 2 listed building as are also a number of houses in the High Street. These all lie close together and make a picturesque corner. A little further on is a little garden set aside to house the old market cross and village stocks. It is a pleasant corner with some new garden seats. As so often, the cross is a rather pathetic stump, and at the time of writing, the stocks have been taken away, presumably for repair. The village lies on the B6391 which leaves the A660 Bolton-Darwen road at Bromley Cross.

CHATTERTON AND STRONGSTRY, ROSSENDALE. These two places are hardly villages, just rather isolated rows of stone built weavers cottages on the banks of the River Irwell. At Chatterton the mill remains as well. There is quite a rural atmosphere about the place and they are best visited by a short (30-40 min.) walk from Stubbins. Start at the Railway Hotel, go under the railway bridge, and turn right. Continue along the road leading to Stubbins Vale Mill and follow it until you come to the old railway on your right. Go under the bridge and just ahead on your left is the double row of cottages of Strongstry. Continue along the pleasant riverside path to the first foot-bridge, cross it and continue along the minor road through the hamlet of Chatterton until you meet the A56. Turn left on it and a few minutes will see you back to your starting point. Stubbins lies on the A676 just north of Ramsbottom.

EDGWORTH, BOLTON. The conservation Area in this long drawn out village is at the bottom of the hill, near Turton Bottoms, not where the name Edgworth appears on the map. The bulk of the houses are up the hill, and there are a number of very fine old ones, such as those in Isherwood Fold, and Brandwood Fold, built in 1650, but the village atmosphere is diminished by the large housing estate. Lower down along Bolton road are the pub, the Spread Eagle, the old Methodist School built in 1828, and a large number of other grade 2 listed buildings. Though very extended, Edgworth probably has as many fine buildings and interesting 'corners' as anywhere in the Area. It stands on a minor road that runs from the B6391 at Chapeltown to B6232 Blackburn-Haslingden road.

HODDLESDEN, DARWEN. This hill top village built around Queens Street and Queens Square owes its present form to the twin Victorian pillars of coal and cotton. Once the centre of a considerable colliery activity, it had a special branch line built from the Darwen-Bolton railway line to transport its coal.

Today just a fragment can be seen at the bottom of the hill. Two of its old mills remain, still in use. The village's principle attraction lies in its compactness and its freedom from modern intrusions. Perhaps the most attractive feature is the pair of symmetrically gabled rows of houses in a late Georgian style bearing words in Latin: BUILT BY O. HARGREAVE, 1844. Holker House Farm is worth a short walk to look at. Park by the Congregational church and turn left before the road climbs steeply up to the village. Turn left at the next T junction, and the house is in sight about 100 yards away. Time: 5-10 minutes. From this point you can see the remains of the railway track that went up to the colliery on Grey Stone Hill. Can be approached along minor roads from either Darwen or Blackburn.

Holcombe

HOLCOMBE, RAMSBOTTOM. The area included here is quite large and extends up to the Monument on the moor. The most picturesque corner lies along the bridleway, lined with elegant old houses, rather than weavers cottages. Further along the bridleway is Hey House and the Aitken Sanatorium, formerly

Holcombe Hall. Walk No. 3, Section 3, takes you through this area. It lies along the old Haslingden-Bury road, B6214.

IRWELL VALE, ROSSENDALE. The Rossendale valley, the once beautiful valley of the River Irwell, ravaged in the early days of the Industrial Revolution, here retains something of its rural charm. Situated at the end of the road between the R. Irwell and the R. Ogden, there is little room for development and the community of mill workers cottages has stayed intact. It is best approached from Ewood Bridge on the A680 Haslingden-Ramsbottom road.

RIDING GATE, HARWOOD, BOLTON. This quaint corner is not named on the map as such, it's really a street name, but it is very close to Side of the Moor which is shown on the map. In an area swamped with new housing estates this road contrives to retain an air of seclusion and contains some fine large houses. The Conservation Area includes a fair amount of the pastures around. It is best reached by taking the Tottington road from the B6196 at Harwood Lee and turning left just past the Methodist Chapel.

WALLSUCHES, HORWICH. The Conservation Area takes its name from the former bleach works, but it is more extensive than one would at first suppose. The former bleach works are now occupied by an engineering firm and have recently been cleaned and painted. Bleach works were once a common and important part of the Lancashire scene, many have fallen into disuse and become completely ruinous. This one, thanks to a new use, has been well cared for. Some of the buildings, in particular the old engine house, are impressively designed and built. A datestone in the mill gives a date of 1858. A right-of-way footpath runs through the centre of the buildings and they can easily be inspected on a short walk.

Park in the lay-by opposite the Jolly Crofters, which lies on the B6226, the Bolton-Horwich old road. Take the cinder track past a short row of stone cottages. One of them has the date 1803. The track continues through the works, passing what looks like the original manager's or owner's house. It meets another track coming up from Horwich and which leads to a metalled road and some modern houses. Turn right here and follow it past the reservoir banking. Here is a very fine house indeed, Markland House, with a date stone 1773. Turn right on the footpath here and follow it past some small reservoirs to the cinder track that takes you back to your car in a couple of minutes. Time: 30-40 minutes.

Part Two

WALKS

INTRODUCTION

Terrain of this sort lends itself to recreational walking and its use over the years has produced a network of footpaths as well as the old farm and mine tracks. Many footpaths marked on the maps have disappeared, mainly through lack of use; some have been closed by building; some wired up by farmers; some have been afforested; some have become so overgrown with rushes that they can no longer be walked. The showing of a path on the map is no guarantee that it is still there. Equally, other paths, particularly round the urban fringe, have been 'improved' and are no longer attractive. Local authorities have sign-posted quite a number of tracks where they leave the road, but this is no guarantee that the path continues, that it is easy to follow, or that it goes anywhere worth while. Conversely, some good paths and walks are not marked at all. This book collects together the most interesting walks, and in the notes that follow each walk, gives some account of the natural history, geology, archaeology and architectural features seen on that walk as they are relevant. Once some experience has been gained, it is easy to extend or alter the walks described, but it should be remembered that many footpaths are not sufficiently used to be easily followed and care is needed in walking them to avoid trespass. Unless otherwise stated, all paths used in the book are either rights-of-way or go over land where there is free access. For easy reference the walks in this book are grouped into four sections:—

Section 1. Walks around Anglezarke and Rivington.
Section 2. Walks around Bolton and Bury.
Section 3. Walks around Helmshore, Haslingden, and Holcombe.
Section 4. Walks around Darwen and Tockholes.

Each section has a sketch map showing the parking places mentioned in the text. Road side parking should not be used if at all possible because of congestion and the problems it causes to those whose daily business rather than pleasure takes them onto the roads.

The use of the new second series 1/25,000 map, sheet S.D.61/71 Bolton (North) is most strongly recommended. It covers sections 1 and 2 which comprise the greater part of the Area. Unfortunately sheet S.D.62/72 which will cover the northern part, has not yet been published, and only the first series sheets S.D.62 Darwen and S.D.72 Accrington are available. These two maps are rather out of date and do not show rights of way as such nor footpaths in colour. They are not nearly so easy to use as the second series maps. The old one inch map Sheet 95 (Blackburn) covers sections 3 and 4 and half of 1. Sheet 101 covers the rest. In the new 1/50,000 series maps the relevant sheets are 103 and 109. The 1/25,000 maps shows the position of the museums, some Ancient Monuments and listed buildings, and enables the Conservation Areas to be located. The place names used in the text are as used on this map except where local tradition has used other names. Then these are given as well.

Boots are recommended for all moorland walks, but a great many of the others are suitable for shoes especially in summer. The times given are for people accustomed to walking. Family parties will need longer, good walkers less time. The times given do not allow a lot of time for stopping and looking around. Whilst most of the walks have been chosen as circular tours, some of the best are 'point to point' walks for which local bus services are useful. Ring Bolton 32131, Darwen 72765, Blackburn 51112, or Rossendale 7777 for details of corporation bus times in the various sections. Ribble also run bus services through the Area. Their local offices: Blackburn 54369, Burnley 23125, Bolton 21021, Chorley 2247, will supply bus times.

In bad weather, and especially in winter, care should be exercised on the remoter moorland walks. Unless you are an experienced hillwalker with a knowledge of map and compass it is better to keep to the well marked paths unless conditions are good. An anorak and overtrousers will help keep out wind and rain, and a spare sweater is always useful. In winter, woollen gloves and something to keep your ears warm, like a balaclava, are necessary. A torch and spare bar of chocolate are useful accessories in winter, too — in case you are caught by the short winter days!

If you come by car it is a good idea to have a simple change of clothing in the car. After a wet day it can make the drive home much more comfortable.

On summer evenings beware of the midges in some of the quarries such as Lester Mill — they are positively ferocious!

Finally, as the County Council is administering the Area with conservation strongly in mind, be conservation minded yourself. Do nothing that will injure your environment. Do nothing that will interfere with other people's enjoyment of the countryside, and do nothing that will hinder the efforts of the people who make a living from the land you enjoy visiting. To be more specific:—

1. Take all your litter home with you.
2. When picnicking use a gas stove, not a fire.
3. Be careful with your matches and cigarettes. Remember the devastating fires on the moors in the summer of 1980. Their effects can still be seen.
4. Enjoy the flowers and trees where they are growing.
5. Remember that most streams run into reservoirs for drinking water and take care not to pollute them.
6. Close all gates so that animals cannot stray onto the road.
7. In lambing time keep your dog on a lead. A sheep in lamb that is chased by a dog and not even touched by it is liable to lose that lamb.
8. Take care not to block farm gates and access roads when you park. If at all possible use the recommended parking places for these walks.
9. Wherever possible use stiles to cross walls and fences.

Whilst this book is primarily a guide to the excellent walking in the Area, there are many other recreational possibilities. Of a less strenuous nature are visits to the local museums mentioned in Part One, each depicting in its own special way, life as it was lived or worked in times past. Including these museums, there are eleven Ancient Monuments, a number of Conservation Areas and a wealth of listed buildings.

In addition there are a large number of club-orientated leisure pursuits. Many of the reservoirs have their fishing rights let out to local angling clubs. Hang gliding is carried out in suitable weather from Winter Hill and radio controlled gliders are flown from several places around Rivington Pike. Though there are not many bridleways in the Area, some riding is done round Rivington. Sailing is carried on on the Belmont, Delph, and Jumbles reservoirs, and there is canoeing on the Blue Lagoon at Belmont. Rock climbing is practised at Cadshaw and many of the quarries. Orienteering and cross country runs take place in the moorland parts and there is an annual race up Rivington Pike and a race around the Three Towers. As yet water ski-ing and skin diving are not permitted in the reservoirs, but it is evident that, leaving aside the wide fields for ornithological and botanical studies, there is a wealth of leisure opportunity in the Area.

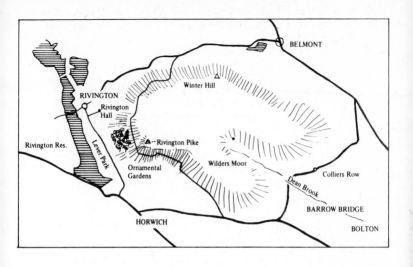

1. WALKS AROUND ANGLEZARKE AND RIVINGTON

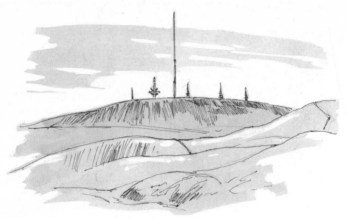

Winter Hill

THE ASCENT OF WINTER HILL WALK NO. **1.1**

Ascent is rather a grand word to use for a mere hill, but at a
height of 1498 feet, or 456 metres, Winter Hill is the highest
point in the West Pennine Moors Area. There are several ways
of making the ascent. Best are:—
1.   From the highest point of the Rivington — Belmont road.
This is short and sharp.
Time: 30 min. to the top, 1 hr.-1 hr. 30 min. for the circuit.
2.   From Belmont. This is the nicest way on a fine morning
and the best for shoes.
Time: 1 hr. to the top, 2 hrs. for the circuit.
3.   From Rivington Pike. Have boots or wellies or wet feet.
Time: ¾ hr. from the Pike or 1 hr. 35 min. from the road end
for the round walk.
4.   From the Scout Road. Longest in distance, but a gentle
ascent easy to follow.
Time: 1 hr. to the top, 2 hrs. for the circuit.

1.   From the top of the Rivington — Belmont road
There's room to park there. The track runs direct from the road
by the wall to the masts. It's pretty wet in parts and disappears
just as you need it most, that's to say, when it gets steep. Just
engage bottom gear and grunt slowly on. The Ordnance Survey
cairn is just to the left, before you get to the masts. If visibility is
good, the view can be very wide — see Walk No. 2 for a

description of the views to the west. To the north Great Hill is only a couple of miles away; beyond it the Bowland Fells stand clear. Further right, Pendle, Penyghent, Ingleborough and Whernside can be seen occasionally. Darwen Tower is unmistakable and always on view, but industrial haze often hides Holcombe Tower, the other one of the three hill top towers in the Area. It's a fine moorland walk to visit all three in the day. (See the last walk.) Between Darwen and Holcombe Towers is featureless moorland, difficult to identify unless there's fog in the valleys and the tops are clear, a rare state of affairs occuring only in winter.

Instead of returning as you came, it makes a pleasant extension of the walk to go along the edge of the moor towards the sea. A little track starts just past the masts and runs to the tumulus that can be seen as a pip on the moor. When you come to the boggy hollow (full of cotton grass in June), bear left a little and find the driest way you can. At the tumulus you wil! see the rough road that runs round the Pike about 100 yards away. Turn right on it and a further 20 minutes will see you back to you car.

The Blue Lagoon, Belmont

2.   From Belmont village

Convenient parking is a bit of a problem. The track starts almost opposite the Wright Arms, ½ mile on the Bolton side of the village. There's parking there for customers, so maybe you first fortify yourself and later refresh yourself! Otherwise find a back street or go up to the Blue Lagoon on the Rivington road. There, at least, it is convenient for the return if you do the circular walk.

From the pub, cross the road, and take the track that starts in the corner of the fir plantation. It goes right through it and then slants to the right, climbing gently all the way to the top. There's a garden seat about three quarters of the way up if you're flagging. Once on the tarmac at the top, turn right and go boldly on through the gate and look for the cairn on the right before you pass the masts. Either retrace your steps or descend the steep slope overlooking the road. It's best to go a good 100 yards further on than the cairn before descending. Take care on this. If you fall, you're liable to roll or slide — unpleasant. Once on the road, turn right and follow it back to Belmont. Not very far down there's a little foot-path on the right that leads very pleasantly to the Blue Lagoon. A branch of it goes to the right of the Lagoon and crosses a couple of little bridges to get back to the road. Then it's road all the way if you're parked at the pub.

3. From Rivington Pike

To get the best out of this walk, go on a sunny evening in a dry spell, otherwise, unless you've got good boots, you'll get very wet feet. If you want the shortest possible approach to the Pike, turn up Georges Lane, Horwich. It leaves the B6226 almost opposite the Jolly Crofters, becomes very rough but is motorable. You can stop just below the Pike which is about 10 minutes walk, very steep at the front, but easier round the back. It is a splendid view point on a clear evening.

From the top of the Pike a broad squelchy track leads straight to the T.V. masts. It will take longer than you think, and when you reach the road made of railway sleepers cross it and continue to the tarmac road. Follow this past the T.V. station and the Scotsman's Stump. Where the road ends by the Police radio masts, go boldly on, and you will find the cairn on the right before you've passed the masts. Now follow the little path to the tumulus (see route no. 1) and there keep straight on down (steep) to the rough road. Turn left on this, and about 20 min. will see you back at your car. If you don't care to drive that extremely rough road, park where the tarmac ends and walk along it instead. Then it is better to return as follows: From the T.V. Station follow the tarmac road down towards Horwich until it starts to bend to the left and you can see a big stone cairn straight ahead. You will see a broad but rather faint track going off to the right. Follow this down to Pike Cottage, turn left, and a few minutes sees you back.

*Rivington Pike from the path
to Winter Hill.*

4. From the Scout Road

The Scout Road is the narrow moorland road joining the
B6226 at the Bob Smithy Inn with the A675 near the Wilton
Arms. Smithills Dean Road joins the Scout Road at about half
way. Across from Smithills Dean Road is an unclassified road
which can be used to start the walk. With a car, however, if the
circular walk is to be undertaken it is better to park at Colliers
Row, near Brownstones Quarry, about a half mile west of the
crossroads.

Follow the unmade road by the side of the cottages, pass the farm and turn right. Turn left on the tarmac road. The house on the left below the road was the inspiration for 'Grimsdyke', a children's novel by Walt Unsworth, set in these moors (though the actual site was Hempshaw's on the Anglezarke Moor). Where the road forks keep to the right. After a bit a stile is crossed and the road becomes a path. Quite distinct and easy to follow to the masts.

To return, go down the road from the masts until a track is seen on the left leading down into Dean Brook, the broad valley on the left. Good at first the path is hard to follow in the middle but soon recovers and becomes a good bridle path leading to Walker Fold. Turn left up the road and five minutes walk brings you back to Colliers Row.

Notes about Winter Hill

Winter Hill owes its steep northern slope to faulting and subsequent weathering of the fault. All of Winter Hill is typical moorland containing many boggy places. Cotton grass grows in the wettest places, an indication to avoid them if you can. One relatively rare and interesting plant of the wet places is the cranberry. There's a big patch of it on top, but I'll not tell you just where. In any case, it produces far too few berries to make any luscious cranberry sauce.

Winter Hill has been the scene of man's handiwork since pre-historic times. There is a neolithic burial mound about ¼ mile west of the cairn, but today it has practically disappeared. It is thought to date to 1500 B.C. Of greater interest to archaeologists is the tumulus that I described as a 'pip on the moor'. This is the Noon Hill Ring Cairn. It has been excavated and a shattered burial urn was recovered and has been restored and placed in Bolton Municipal Museum.

Much later, coal was mined and the remains of old coal pits can be seen here and there. There is one, now fenced round, near the road by the Post Office Mast, and there are many others. They were worked in the late 18th and early 19th centuries, and are known as 'bell pits'. On the moors the coal seams are close to the surface and the winning of coal did not present the technical problems that deeper though more readily accessible pits would have done.

The Scotsman's Stump is a memorial to one James Henderson, a native of Annan, Dumfriesshire, who was brutally murdered on Nov. 9th 1803, on Rivington Moor. He was a pedlar, travelling from Wigan or Blackrod to Belmont and Blackburn. At that time this was the most direct road between those places.

Later still came technological man. The police masts near the O.S. cairn were the first of all the masts to be built in 1948, then followed the first T.V. mast in 1955, soon to be replaced by the present tubular mast which is over 1000 ft. (328 metres) high. The P.O. mast was built in 1955. Truly, man has made use of these moors!

Notes about Rivington Pike
Rivington Pike, 1198 ft. or 365 metres high, is known to have been the site of an ancient beacon, one of a chain of signal fires used to send warnings in time of danger. It is said to have been in use by 1138 A.D., and there is a written record that it was lit on July 1st 1588, when the Armada was sailing up the Channel. The Tower was built in 1733 on the beacon platform, using some of the stones. Originally it had a roof, doors and windows, and was used as a shooting lodge at one time. It fell into disrepair and was wilfully damaged, but it has now been restored. It is a Grade 2 listed building.

Rivington Pike

The Pike is the best place for late evening and sunset views in the whole Area. Go there some clear summer evening, preferably a Saturday when there is less industrial smoke, and contrive to be on the Pike about an hour before sunset. Then, if you have a bit of luck, the evening sky will be bright, the sea will be lit up, and the hills of North Wales and the Lake District will be silhouetted against the sea, giving the best possible conditions of long distance viewing. See the previous walk for instructions on how to get to the Pike.

Having got there, what can you expect to see? As far left as possible, where the view is cut off by Rivington Moor, you can just make out the outline of the Staffordshire Hills, but the first bold one on the left is HELSBY HILL, 35 miles away, and seen right behind the cooling towers of the power station at Fiddlers Ferry. Slightly to its right stands the long undulating range of the CLWYDIAN HILLS which separate Mold and Denbigh. They are 45 miles away and you can see them quite often. To their right, between the nearby Harrock Hill and Ashurst Beacon (you can see the beacon through binoculars), is Snowdonia itself, or more precisely, the CARNEDDAU. They apparently end where GT. ORME dips into the sea. This is 60 miles away. Even further to the right, a full 80 miles away, and only seen if conditions are really good, is the tip of ANGLESEY. Sometimes, if the sea is well lighted, you can see the whole of the coast-line of Liverpool Bay.

Coming much nearer home is the gasometer at Southport, then you can see the Ribble and its tributary that rises on Winter Hill, the Douglas. Then follows BLACKPOOL TOWER and the elevators at Fleetwood. Across Morecambe Bay is the whaleback of BLACK COMBE, most westerly of the Lakeland Hills and quite often seen. It's 55 miles away. A mass of undulating high ground separates it from the next distinctive pair of hills, DOW CRAG and CONISTON OLD MAN, and at the other end of that block of rather higher ground, you can see the shoulder of BOWFELL dipping in to Langdale. The LANGDALE PIKES themselves can only just be seen, they're so small, but the drop to Dunmail Raise and the climb to HELVELLYN is visible. Then the nearer BOWLANDS cut off any further views to the right. It's a truly wonderful panorama.

These long distance views will very likely make you ask, "Why couldn't I see the Isle of Man?", and, "Just how far can I see when it's really clear"? It's very difficult to answer these questions simply. The distance depends very much on how clear 'really clear' is. Moisture is always present in our atmosphere to some extent, and it is never as clear here as in the Alps or Himalaya. There are five other important points:—

1. The height you are above sea level.
2. The height of the mountain or other object you are looking at.
3. The curvature of the earth.
4. Refraction.
5. The difference in brightness between the object you are looking at and its background, and, obviously, its size.

If you are 1000 ft. above sea level then you can see the horizon at sea level 41.83 miles away. At 2000 ft. this increases to 59.20 miles. Obviously if you're looking at high mountains like Snowdonia you will be able to see them further away than the horizon itself. The thing whose effect is difficult to calculate is refraction. Refraction is the bending of rays of light around the earth and has the effect of enabling you to see round the curvature of the earth, as it were, and observe even more distant objects. An extreme case is the mirage in the desert. As the effect of refraction depends upon the temperature of the air, you can see how difficult it is to estimate its effect. The difference in brightness or optical contrast doesn't so much affect the distance you can see, but rather whether or not your eye can pick out the object you're looking for. It's much the same thing in the long run.

This was demonstrated quite strikingly one day when I was returning to Hayfield from a walk over Kinder Scout. It was a dull day, and though the moorlands were clear we could not see the T.V. mast to identify Winter Hill with certainty. Then a patch of bright sky appeared in the west and rapidly spread. Suddenly we could see the mast, sharp and clear as a giant needle silhouetted against the bright sky.

In theory it should be possible to see Snowdon standing above the Carneddau, as it is 300 ft. higher than them. In practice the light is always too uniform and 300 ft. is barely sufficient to see at that distance. It ought to be possible to see the Isle of Man, though at 95 miles distant it is considerably more than any of the hills listed. I have never seen it despite many good clear evenings on the Pike. I have, however, seen St. Bees Head, the most westerly point of Cumbria, from North Wales, and that is an incredible 110 miles away, but Rivington Pike was too small to be seen and was lost against the back-

43

ground of the moors. St. Bees juts out into the sea and was clear and unmistakable. It seems that we need unusual conditions of the atmosphere to see the Isle of Man.

Now if you have a half inch or similar Merseyside map, just have a look at it. You will see that a line drawn on the map from the Pike to the Menai Straits shows that the Straits cannot be seen as a clear gap between the mainland and the island of Anglesey. Yet you could see a very large gap indeed, perfectly clearly. This is because the sea is forming the horizon considerably closer than the Menai Straits, and Anglesey and Snowdonia are seen further away partly because they are higher and partly because of refraction.

A VISIT TO THE RIVINGTON ORNAMENTAL GARDENS

These gardens, part of Viscount Leverhulme's Rivington Estates, were planned on a vast scale along a steep hillside, and are sometimes called the Terrace Gardens or Chinese Gardens. Today only those plants and trees with a robust constitution survive. A very rough public road runs diagonally through the gardens, climbing up from Horwich to where there was once an entrance, and then dropping to meet the Rivington — Belmont road. The two parts are linked by an elegant stone footbridge.

You don't need detailed instructions to enjoy these gardens. It is one of their special pleasures to find out what lies round the next corner or up the next flight of steps. You can easily spend a whole afternoon wandering around, and then you may not have seen everything. It's a place that repays many visits. It is probably best to park at Rivington Hall Barn to explore the lower part. To find this take the Rivington road from Horwich just below the round-about at the junction of the B6226 and the A675. At Great House Barn, take the avenue on the right straight to Rivington Hall and Barn.

Leave the car park behind the barn, keep to the right of the cottage and take the lane that winds up the hill. In about 100 yards you will come in sight of an open meadow with swing gate. Go through this, follow the path up the field to the next stile and enter the woods of the Bungalow Gardens, yet another name for them. Do not be in a hurry to climb upward and you will come to the start of one of several magnificent stone staircases climbing the hillside. Close by is a deep cut 'fairy dell' with man made pools, waterfalls and grottoes. Work your way upwards to the rough road that divides the gardens, and turn left on it until you come to the foot-bridge. Here, a very steep narrow set of steps not a staircase, will bring you back to the bottom, but in between are many level paved paths and other sets of steps that give enjoyable wandering.

You can best visit the upper and more interesting part by parking at the end of the short metalled road that branches off the Rivington-Belmont road just below Moses Cocker Farm (parking difficult at week-ends). Walk along this road to the bridge mentioned above, and enter the gardens by the splendid staircase that starts from it. Originally, of course, there was no access from this road, but the passage of many feet has worn a clear track to its lower end. Take the climb slowly. Enjoy the view from the arbours so conveniently built for this purpose.

The Dove Cote and the Ornamental Gardens

High on the left is the tower that was originally a dovecote. Below, to its right, is a fish pond at one time fed by a spring cascading down the hill. Away to the right is a pergola where there was a rose garden, and below it, across one of the main access roads to the Bungalow, the remains of the kitchen gardens, still partly walled for shelter, yet in the sun. Below these and further right still are the poor remains of the once exotic Oriental Garden. Gone are the pagoda-like buildings and the footbridge that created a scene reminiscent of that on a willow pattern plate.

The Bungalow itself, the heart of the fine gardens, where was that? It was built quite high up, not far below the Pike. The original one was a timber and tile affair, the very essence of a bungalow in appearance, and it was burnt down by Suffragettes on 7th July 1913. This was ironical, as Viscount Leverhulme was not unsympathetic to their cause. However, without delay he had the site cleared and built a very substantial "Ye Olde" type bungalow in stone. It was L shaped and stood on the top one of a pair of lawns, the lower one enclosed by the corner of the L. A fine quadrant shaped flight of stairs still stands in this

46

corner connecting the two lawns and will help you to identify the place. On the top lawn a few coloured tiles are all that remain of that once palatial bungalow. What happened to it?

It's a sad story indeed, and coupled with the neglect of the once wonderful gardens, an even sadder comment on the value we placed on our environment in 1945-1950. Admittedly, there were more pressing problems then. When Viscount Leverholme died, the estates were sold to a Mr. Magee of Bolton, and on his death to Liverpool Corporation. It would seem likely that they bought them in order to consolidate their position as a principle landowner with an especial responsibility for the purity of the water they supplied. They must have found the Bungalow something of a white elephant and expensive to maintain. A conference of local authorities called in 1947 to discuss possible uses of the Bungalow failed to agree to any solution, and the Corporation subsequently demolished it and allowed the gardens to be despoiled. By 1970 or thereabouts, the climate of public opinion had changed and work was started to open up the paths and restore the decaying stonework. Rhododendrons and sapling trees had made such vigorous growth that the place was a veritable jungle, penetrable only by small boys creeping Red Indian fashion along tunnels in the undergrowth.

Today, in 1977, the major terraces and connecting steps and staircases have been cleared of overhanging trees and shrubs. Many staircases, arbours, and the pergola have been truly restored in matching stonework. Some archways and flights of stairs have been excavated from accumulated debris, and in 1976 the Dovecote, a Grade 2 listed building, was re-roofed. Two ponds have been excavated but do not at present, seem to be holding water too well. All this work, much of it real hard graft, has been carried out by parties of volunteers working under the supervision of the National Conservation Corps and the British Trust for Conservation who were given a grant by the N.W.W.A. in 1975. Their efforts, which are still continuing, have now made the gardens a splendid place in which to wander at all times of the year. We can only marvel at the sort of place it once was for it is clearly not practicable to restore them fully. A collection of old photographs in Chorley Reference Library give just an inkling of the place in its pomp and glory.

A STROLL AROUND LEVER PARK   WALK NO. **1.4**

Lever park is no extension of a town park but a great chunk of varied and open countryside, once part of Lord Leverhulme's Rivington Estates, and still bearing signs of his handiwork. Today it has been designated a country park. You can find it very easily from Horwich, taking the road to Rivington which leaves the A673 just below the roundabout near the Crown Hotel. About a mile along that road, just past the Grammar School, there is a car park on the left. Of course, it's not far to walk all the way from the bus stop at the Crown.

Time: about 1½ hours, but plenty of variations are possible.

From the car park a tree lined unmetalled road leads to the Rivington Castle, an imitation ruin built on the shore of the Lower Rivington reservoir. It's well worth a look round even though a fence prevents access to the shore. Two other tree lined avenues lead back to the metalled road the most obvious one joins it just before Great House Barn, where refreshments are available. From here, there is a fine view of Rivington Hall at the end of its avenue of trees. Continue along the metalled road for a little way, then take the first unmetalled avenue to the left. This runs down to the shore of the reservoir and joins the road again in Rivington Village by the school. The church is on the knoll opposite. Turn right and right again at the village green, pausing to look at the Unitarian Chapel with its Garden of Rest most pleasantly tucked away behind the Chapel's schoolroom. Continue along the road and take the first unmetalled road on the left. This leads to Rivington Hall Barn, open for refreshments every day. Leave by the back of the Barn, pass to the right of the cottage and take the lane that climbs up the hill until it meets yet another unmetalled road. Turn right on this and follow it until it crosses another one. Go straight ahead, and the metalled road lies about 200 yards ahead. Turn left, and 10 minutes will see you within sight of your car. There are a number of other unmetalled roads within the park, mostly motorable, though very rough, but they do give a lot of easy walking suitable for shoes and any weather. You won't need any more directions.

Notes about Lever Park and the buildings in it.

A pair of granite pillars mark the entrance to Lever Park Avenue, Horwich, the left hand one of which bears the following inscription:

LEVER PARK
THE GIFT OF
WILLIAM HESKETH LEVER
1st VISCOUNT LEVERHULME
BORN AT 6 WOOD STREET BOLTON
SEPTEMBER 19th 1861
DIED AT HAMPSTEAD LONDON
MAY 7th 1925
FOR THE BENEFIT OF THE CITIZENS
OF HIS NATIVE TOWN AND NEIGHBOURHOOD
BY ACT OF PARLIAMENT IN 1902 THE
OWNERSHIP AND CARE OF THE PARK
WERE VESTED IN THE
CORPORATION OF THE CITY OF LIVERPOOL

This, in a nutshell, is the story of Lever Park, the Rivington Bungalow, and the Ornamental Gardens. Mr. W. H. Lever amassed a huge fortune in producing a soap that was far better than any available at the time. It was known as Sunlight Soap, a household word even today. His chemist's skill in formulating the soap and his own business acumen laid the foundations of a company that eventually became the world-wide Unilever.

He bought Rivington Hall and manor in 1900. The estate included land which is now known as Lever Park. At once he started to indulge in his passion for fresh air and gardens, building the bungalow and the ornamental terrace gardens below the Pike. He acquired a collection of animals such as fallow deer, zebu, emus and wallabies, and kept them in the park in the open air behind stout iron fences, a number of which remain. In 1901 Mr. Lever most generously attempted to give a large part of his estates to the citizens of Bolton, but because of legal wrangles with Liverpool Corporation, the procedure noted on the pillar was required.

The Ornamental Gardens, though open to the public today (See Walk No. 3) were not part of the original gift of land. The Pike, however, was included in the original gift, and included land above the 1,250 ft. contour, and wide access to it from the high road. This must surely have been one of the earliest gifts of hill country ever made to the people of the British Isles. Shortly afterwards Mr. Lever became 1st Viscount Leverhulme.

Rivington Castle with its three approaches of tree lined avenues was perhaps Viscount Leverhulme's only 'folly'. Eccentric he may have been, generous to a degree, and even this replica of Liverpool Castle, a ruin on Liverpool Bay, was an idea for the benefit of the public that was never completed. There should have been a terrace cafe, set in rose gardens, overlooking the lake. How delightful that would have been today!

Rivington is quite an ancient village. It lost its pub but little else when the Lower Rivington Reservoir was built. The school, now only for juniors, was founded in 1566 by Bishop Pilkington, third son of Richard Pilkington of Rivington Hall. The present building dates from 1714 and is on the original site. The Church has no special features and has been rebuilt a number of times. The Unitarian Chapel, a rather austere building, is one of the earliest in Lancashire, dating back to 1703. There are stones bearing considerably earlier dates in its graveyard. The present Rivington Hall is a late Georgian building replacing in 1780 an earlier Tudor structure, and the site is much older than that. It is noted in Domesday Book, and it is thought that in Saxon times there was a manor there.

Support for this belief is seen in the construction of the Hall Barn. It is cruick built with massive oaken timbers supported on low stone pillars, a very unusual form of construction in Lancashire, used from late Saxon times for many centuries. The Hall Barn is thought to have been built around 1500 A.D. Never easy to date a building of the type, it is now infinitely more difficult because of the 'restoration' carried out by Viscount Leverhulme between 1900 and 1910. This was virtually a conversion to a mock Tudor dance hall-cum-tea room, a travesty of restoration as it is carried out today. The best that can be said of it is that the ancient roof structure was retained and repaired with old oak and that the building was given a new lease of life that enables it to survive today. There is a photograph in the Chorley Library's collection of the interior as it was before restoration. It can be seen quite clearly that then there were no side aisles. Great House Barn, known locally as the Little Barn has a similar construction and was restored at the same time. The Little Barn has only two pairs of cruicks or roof trusses, instead of six in the Hall Barn, and it is much smaller. The Hall Barn is over 100 ft. long, 57 ft. wide and almost 25 ft. at the point of the roof. Both the Hall Barn and Great House Barn are Grade 1 listed buildings. The Hall, Castle, Church and Chapel are Grade 2 listed buildings. The school is Grade 3.

A WALK ROUND THREE ARCHAEOLOGICAL
SITES AT RIVINGTON   WALK NO. 1.5

It is an unfortunate fact that many archaeological remains in the Area have been buried, destroyed or otherwise lost. In the case of the Twa Lads burial mounds on Wilders Moor and the tumulus on Winter Hill little remains except heaps of stones and patches of a different kind of vegetation. The remains at Noon Hill Slack, an outlier of Winter Hill, fortunately give something worth looking at.

The best approach is to drive up Georges Lane, Horwich, which starts opposite the Jolly Crofters on the B6226, just south of Horwich. After a lot of potholes the metalled section ends. It's easy to park there.

Time: 1½-2 hours.

Continue along the rough road to Pike Cottage and there take the footpath that goes up the moor. It keeps left of the true top of the Twa Lads Moor, but make a diversion to the top when it is within easy reach. The big cairn there is more or less on the site of the twin burial mounds and a later Iron Age fort, but little or nothing remains that can be identified with any certainty.

Return to the path and follow it to the tarmac road leading to the T.V. station. Go diagonally left at the end of the Station buildings, aiming for the P.O. mast. There is a little path that cuts the corner and passes some of the old coal pits which abound on Winter Hill. Go through the gate across the road, pass the police masts and continue on a well marked path that slopes gently down to Noon Hill Slack. Don't rush it. Start looking on the left, right up against the track about 300 yards from the fence for the next tumulus site. It's a patch of very green grass with a lot of stone around the edge, and it's easier to see looking up the hill than down it. Having found it, continue along the path to Noon Hill Slack, easily seen as a pip on the moor straight ahead. Avoid the wet hollow as best you can by keeping to the left. The unusual structure of the tumulus can easily be seen. Again follow the same little track straight ahead down to the rough road that runs around the Pike, where a left turn will take you back to your car in about 30 minutes and give you fine south westward views all the way.

Archaeological Notes

The Twa Lads was originally a Bronze Age twin cairn — hence the name. It has not been excavated in modern times but was opened up in the seventeenth century and all evidence lost. Until fairly recently a heap of stones marked the spot. It seems likely that they have been removed to build the fine cairn on top of Wilders Moor, only a short distance away. Thus is archaeological evidence lost for ever. Were it not that the site is known, and listed, it would soon be forgotten.

The tumulus just west of the summit on Winter Hill was excavated in 1958 by Manchester University and Chorley Archaeological Society, whose report is filed in Chorley Library. The mound had been opened at some time unknown and the remains removed. It was thought to date to about 1500 B.C. that is to say, Early Bronze Age. Evidently any restoration work was quite inadequate, for today little remains.

The Ring Cairn on Noon Hill Slack was excavated at the same time. It is still quite well seen as a circle 33 ft. in diameter and originally it stood 6 ft. above the moor. It was stone built, covered with turf, and formed a natural amphitheatre. It was used by local Non-conformists as a meeting place in the early days of the break from the established church when it was still illegal to have a church building. The excavation revealed evidence of three burials, some burnt bones, and a broken urn which has been restored and placed in the Bolton Municipal Museum. The whole is thought to date from 1100 B.C.

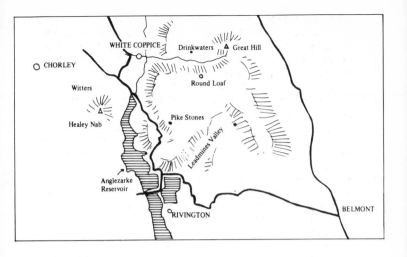

GREAT HILL AND THE ANGLEZARKE MOORS
WALK NO. **1.6**

Great Hill isn't even given a spot height on the map. It's about 365 metres or 1200 ft. high, a good view point, and a very easy climb from White Coppice. It can also be taken in your stride on the two longer walks described here.

Time just to do Great Hill: 1¼-1½ hours return.

To find White Coppice turn off the Chorley-Blackburn road (A675) at Lower Wheelton — it's sign posted Heapey, turn left by the Railway Inn, bear left over the little bridge by the cottages, and turn left into the cinder track. This leads to the cricket field — surely there is no prettier cricket field in the whole of Lancashire — and this together with the setting of the row of old, picturesque cottages by the reservoir make a visit to White Coppice worth while even if you don't want to climb Great Hill. Park by the cricket field or on the wide part of the cinder track.

Cross the Goit by the stone bridge, turn sharp left as soon as you're through the swinging gate, and sharp right at the Ramblers Association sign post. A broad, well-marked track leads you unmistakably to the top. If it's clear the view is similar to that from the Pike, but it's not so easy to see North Wales. On the other hand you can see the Lakes more easily to the left of the Bowlands, and Pendle Hill separating the Ribble and Calder valleys. Darwen Tower cuts off any view further right than this, though you can just see the top part of Bull Hill, the highest part in the eastern section of the West Pennine Moors Area, in the dip between Darwen Moor and Turton Moor. It's not very often the industrial valleys are sufficiently clear of haze and smoke to give these views to the east.

From the top there's a choice of ways back besides just retracing your steps all the way. The most pleasant one is to retrace your steps just to Drinkwaters Farm, the last derelict farm on the way up. At the beginning of the trees you will find a little track going off to the left and leading down to the edge of the stream. There you will find another little track leading right down the stream. It enters a fine little gorge, crosses the stream once or twice, and finally comes out on the steep bit of the hill above White Coppice.

Another way is to retrace your steps just past Drinkwaters to where there is an R.A. sign post to Brinscall. Follow this well-marked cart track across the moor and past the top of a wood. Towards the end of the wood the track forks. Take the left hand branch and follow it down the hill to where it crosses the stream. Here the track forks again. Take the left hand one which enters the woods, and follow it through the woods dropping down gently to meet a track at a bridge over the Goit. Here there is a choice of ways. The easiest is to cross the bridge and go through the gate onto the waterman's track on the other side of the Goit. Leave it at the next gate and bear right a little on to the track that runs round the right hand side of the reservoir and back to White Coppice. This track is not a right of

The Goit at White Coppice

54

way, and you may find the gate locked. In this case don't cross the bridge, but go over the stile opposite. Aim at a row of holly trees and there you will find a little path that will take you back to a bridge over the Goit where you will find yourself in the right place to go round the right hand side of the reservoir just described. Time to come back by this route: about an hour.

A more ambitious circuit goes over Redmonds and Spitlers Edges almost to the Belmont-Rivington road, turns down the infant River Yarrow by a pair of derelict farms, from there crosses over to Lead Mine Valley, and climbs up to Jepsons Gate on the road that runs round Anglezarke, and returns to White Coppice by the Goit woods. Time to return to White Coppice: about 2½ hours.

The details of this are as follows: From the top of Great Hill continue in the direction of Darwen Tower for about 100 yards. Here, on the right, there is a branch track. Take this, cross the fence at the stile and follow the well defined track that runs along the top of the moor to the Rivington-Belmont Road. There's an awkward place if it's wet, a deep cut grough or trench in the peat. It's easier to cross further left, but take care to return to the main track. On a good day this gives first rate moorland walking. When you are coming down the last bit of steepish hill to the road, and you're within a few hundred yards of it, look for a faint track going off to the right. It runs along a ridge 4-5 ft. wide and about a foot high. A different sort of grass grows on it, much shorter and greener than the surroundings. It is important to start correctly or you will find some very hard going over big tussocks.

The ridge soon disappears, but the track runs quite distinctly down to Higher Hempshaw's. Cross the stream just below it, and climb gently up to Lower Hempshaw's. As soon as you have gone through the gateway at the end of the ruined buildings, turn right and immediately go through another gateway in the wall. Follow this wall, ignoring a wide groove in the grass to the right that looks like a cart track. The track you want has disappeared temporarily and it appears better to go straight on, but don't be tempted. In about 200 yards there is another wall and from the gap in it you will see the track quite clearly winding its way across the moor to Simms. In late summer it will be overgrown with tall grass and not be so easy to follow. At Simms a cart track gives well marked going to the next ruined building. Here a diversion to the left *may* avoid an extremely boggy patch in an otherwise good track that leads past old mine spoil heaps into Lead Mine Valley opposite its

War Memorial. Cross the valley and climb up to this by what-
ever path you fancy and leave it by the path that passes to the
right of a hawthorn tree. As you come in sight of the wall you
will see a gap in it. Go through it and follow the path you will
find there to the gate on the Anglezarke road. Turn right and
follow the road past Manor House and Siddow Farm to the
bottom of the hill near the reservoir. There, on the right, is a
swing gate and a track that leads back to White Coppice. It
forks at a bridge over the Goit, but it is better not to cross but to
bear right to the wood, where the path gradually improves all
the way back to White Coppice, and returns you exactly to your
starting point.

Things of Interest Seen on these Moors
There seem to be more derelict farms in this part of the moors
than almost anywhere else. When the district became a water-
works catchment area, all the farms were vacated to avoid any
risk of pollution of the water. Now very little remains of any of
them and it is hard to see how anybody could have made a
living there. Drinkwaters, with its belt of sheltering sycamore
trees is the most prominent. Approaching it, as soon as you are
through the gateway by the R.A. sign post, you can see a row of
mine spoil heaps on the right running down to the stream.
These are the remains of some old shafts dug in the early part of
the nineteenth century to exploit a vein of galena, one of the
ores of lead. A little further on you pass the spring from which
the farm took its water supply, just below on the right. There's
a trough in a recess built of stones in the crevices of which the
little Hard fern grows. Ferns are rare on moorlands because
they need shade and drainage which here are provided by the
recess. Round Loaf can be seen across the stream on the right
from this point. You can visit it on the return trip using the
track from Drinkwaters to the stream, but there is no track up
the other side for quite a way and it's hard going. (See Walk
No. 1.7 for some more information.)

Once you've gone through the top gate you'll see it's mostly
bare peat under foot. This peat layer blankets a large part of
these moors. It only forms in regions of high rainfall — more
than 60 inches (150 cms) — per annum, and low temperatures.
It is formed from decaying vegetation and increases at the rate
of 2 inches (5 cms) per 100 years. Deep layers have been found
to contain pollen grains of birch and alder, sure evidence of a
warmer climate in times past. Today trees will only grow on the
lower slopes or where there is some shelter; for example, the

beech trees by the stream below Drinkwaters. This copse contains quite a variety of trees. There are a few small sycamores, a couple of Scots pines, and a little further down, a willow and a splendid specimen of a rowan or mountain ash. Only the sycamore seems to be sufficiently hardy to grow in the windiest places as at Drinkwaters itself. Black Dean brook cuts quite a little gorge for itself through the soft beds of shale, geologically the same as those in Lead Mine Valley. The War Memorial in Lead Mine Valley was erected by Horwich Rotary Club in memory of the crew of a Wellington bomber that crashed on these moors in 1943.

The Goit is an artificial stream built to bring water from the Roddlesworth reservoir at Tockholes to the Anglezarke reservoir. In its clear waters fingerling trout may sometimes be seen. Dragon flies can sometimes be seen whilst ring ouzel, dipper, and stonechat frequent its banks which are thick with blackberry, meadow sweet and other moisture loving plants. In one place there is a stand of Himalayan Balsam, a very tall plant with thick stems, big leaves and an exotic looking pinkish flower. It seems to be spreading quite fast, though it was once quite rare.

A number of the farms at White Coppice are listed buildings, as are also Manor House Farm and Siddows Farm.

AN ARCHAEOLOGICAL WALK ROUND ANGLEZARKE

This walk goes up one of the nicest wooded valleys in the western part of the moors, visits two of its Ancient Monuments, Round Loaf and Pike Stones, and gives a view of a third one on Noon Hill. Boots are strongly recommended.

Time: about 2 hours.

To find the start of this walk, turn up Babylon Lane at the lights at Adlington, cross the M61 and immediately turn left. Bear right at the Yew Tree Inn and follow the reservoir embankment to a junction marked for the Belmont-Rivington road. Follow this for about ½ mile to where it bends sharply to

Leadmines Valley

cross the Yarrow Reservoir. The walk starts at a swing gate in the corner and it is possible to park there or near it.

The path climbs up Lead Mine Valley, the local name — it's called Limestone Clough on the map. After crossing the stream for the second time the path climbs up to the War Memorial which you will see up on the left. From here several tracks lead in different directions. Take the one that goes up the valley towards the new fence and follow it just below the fence until you can see the main cart track now re-surfaced with unpleasantly large stones as it is an access road in the new afforestation scheme. Join it and follow it up the valley to the derelict shooting hut.

Just before you reach the hut a track climbs up left on to the moor. It used to serve a line of shooting butts. Take it, and after a few minutes you will see Round Loaf ahead, but don't be tempted to make a bee line for it. However wet the track, the moor is worse. Stay on the track until you've crossed the second grough. It can be difficult to cross and is easier up stream. Then make directly for Round Loaf.

The view of Winter Hill with its T.V. masts and Rivington Pike is very good. About half way between the two, on the highest point of the moor, you can just make out as a little pip the tumulus or burial cairn on Noon Hill. Whilst still looking this way, Devil's Dike is the second dark trench across the moor. A wet track goes most of the way to it, and if you decide to go that way, it's best to return direct to the shooting butt track from it.

To visit Pike Stones from here involves a bit of really rough moorland walking. First of all aim at the top of Hurst Hill. There's no path. Choose the side of any convenient drainage ditch, it's usually better going. You won't be able to see Pike Stones from the top of it, but face so that you are walking towards the embankment that separates the Anglezarke and Upper Rivington Reservoirs. If you have a compass take a bearing of 200° from magnetic north. Then 10 minutes walk will see you at Pike Stones.

It used to be possible to follow a little track to a wall corner below you but now that simple route has been cut off by a substantial sheep netting fence topping with barbed wire that surrounds a large area of the moor being afforested. The only way to avoid climbing this fence is to follow it leftwards as you face it until it comes to the cart track in Lead Mine Valley. Then re-trace your steps.

The Waterfall

Things of interest

Soon after crossing the stream in Lead Mine Valley for the first
time you will see that it has cut for itself a little gorge in the
thick bed of crumbling shale. A closer look shows that this
shale is full of what looks like rust. That's exactly what it is,
produced by the weathering of the mineral iron pyrites which is
often found in shale beds. There are a number of old mine spoil
heaps speckled white with barytes, a very heavy mineral, and
the source of barium compounds used in medicine, paper-
making, and today, as an ingredient of the special muds used in
oil well drilling. Towards the end of the 18th century lead was
mined here — hence the local name — and lead is often found
with barytes. In those days there was no use for barytes. Much
higher up this valley, hidden in the oak wood, there is a fine
waterfall, 25-30 ft. high, the highest in the whole Area.

Round Loaf has never been excavated scientifically, but is believed to be a Bronze Age burial mound dating to about 1700-500 B.C. In those times the thick layer of peat that covers the moors had not been laid down because the climate was warmer. The whole area was wooded and much more favourable for habitation by man. Devil's Dike is believed to be some associated earth work, but probably not nearly so old. It is a long shallow trench in the moor, most noticeable because the surrounding heather does not grow in it, only large tufts of grass. Walk No. 1.5 takes you for a closer look at the tumulus on Noon Hill. It is an unusual form built as a hollow ring some 33 ft. in diameter, and originally stood 6 ft. above the level of the moor. It was excavated in 1958, and is thought to date from 1100 B.C.

Pike Stones is a chambered tomb of the Megalithic period (3000-1800 B.C.) It is the oldest man-made object in the Area, and is the only known example of this type of burial mound in the Lancashire Pennines. The tomb has collapsed, but the general form and massive construction can easily be seen.

A WALK ROUND ANGLEZARKE RESERVOIR

This walk is best started from Lester Mill Quarry on the reservoir side, and although you can do it either way round, the paths are easier to find and the views better from the direction given. You can if you like extend it to go round the Upper Rivington Reservoir or you can simply go there for bird watching.

Time: about 2 hours, or 45 minutes to go round the little High Bullough Reservoir.

To find Lester Mill Quarry, turn up Babylon Lane at the lights on the A6, Adlington. Turn right at the first junction and left immediately you've crossed the M61. Take the right fork at the Yew Tree, and very shortly afterwards you will be on the reservoir embankment. Cross it, turn left at the road junction and continue to the new parking ground.

Before starting this walk you may care to spend some time wandering around the little tracks amongst the old quarries on the bracken and heather covered hillside.

When you're ready, follow the tarmac road to the end at the dam on the High Bullough Res. If you now only have time to go around this one, turn right below the dam and follow the track round the other side, crossing a bridge of two enormous slabs of stone. Stay below the wall on the reservoir side and climb on to it in order to step round the end of a wall that runs down the hillside. (A stile has disappeared from here). Turn right on to

Looking over Anglezarke reservoir to Upper and Lower Rivington Reservoirs.

the other dam, cross it and return as you came. The steep steps going up the hill at the end of the dam are the old waterman's steps from the road and are not a right of way.

If you are going round the Anglezarke Reservoir continue along the various tracks that run along the pastures by the reservoir side to the Waterman's Cottage. If you now find yourself short of time it is quicker to return by road from this point. Otherwise continue round the end of the reservoir on the road to its far corner by the wood. Cross the wooden stile and immediatly turn left and follow the track along the wall. This is a good place to watch for duck and other water birds. As the path climbs a little it becomes indistinct. Cross a patch of specially green grass and you will find the path again at the top. It will bring you onto the cart track to Kay's farm and the road. There are very good views from this cart track. Turn left on the road and follow it to the end of the reservoir embankment. Almost opposite a house there is a corner with a gate and stile. Go through this and follow this track first between walls and later divided into a whole lot of animal tracks. Keep to the reservoir side and then follow the wall and it will lead you to a stile onto the road. Then a good 10 minutes along it will see you back to your car.

(Things of interest — see the notes to the next walk.)

A WALK ROUND THE UPPER RIVINGTON AND
YARROW RESERVOIRS   WALK NO. **1.9**

It's immaterial which way round you do this walk and it is suitable for shoes and bad weather.

Time: about 1 hour.

It is probably best to park at the Hall Barn, Rivington, though it is possible to park in odd corners nearer the reservoir. To find the Hall Barn, take the road through Lever Park to Rivington from Horwich, and turn right up a rough road just as you're in sight of the village. If you're coming from the north, turn up Babylon Lane, Adlington, and keep right when you've crossed the M61, take the first turn left and turn right into Rivington village when you've crossed the reservoir bank. The Hall Barn is then up on your left.

Leave the Barn car park by a rough road on the opposite side from the Barn. It takes you to the Belmont-Rivington road where you turn left. Just below the Unitarian Chapel there is a swing gate on the right. From it a pleasant track leads to a set of steps called Forty Steps locally, through there are 41 of them. Go along the stream side to the cinder track that leads to Deane Wood House*. Turn left on this, and as soon as it is through the wall, turn right on the cart track that it meets. This track runs below the Yarrow reservoir. Follow it to the fork, take the left hand branch which leads down to the road by the side of the overflow from the reservoir to the Anglezarke Reservoir. Although it only runs well in times of heavy rain, it is known as the Waterfall. Cross the dam separating the two reservoirs and turn left along the private road that runs down to the Street. It is a public footpath and gives pleasant walking through rhododendron woods. Look for a pet's grave on the right just past a third house. Later there are good views towards the Pike. When you reach the road, turn left and 5 minutes will see you in Rivington village.

Things of interest seen on these two walks

During the retreat of the glaciers at the end of the last Ice Age some 8 or 9 thousand years ago, the water from the melting ice formed a channel between Brinscall and Horwich. Today this is occupied by the Anglezarke and Rivington Reservoirs. These three reservoirs were built in 1850 by Liverpool Corporation, who at the same time, took over Chorley's High Bullough Reservoir and undertook to supply Chorley with water. In 1868 they started the Yarrow Reservoir; small in area but deep. Today, these and all other reservoirs for drinking water are administered by the North West Water Authority. There are many small reservoirs serving former bleach and dye works that are privately owned. Fishing rights are leased to various angling clubs.

The three main reservoirs shelter a big population of wildfowl in winter, especially in the secluded and shallow north eastern part of the Upper Rivington Reservoir. Mallard, tufted and other duck, can often be seen and sometimes wild geese. At sunset on a winter's afternoon, they, together with seagulls, form large rafts in the centre of the Anglezarke Reservoir.

If you arrived by the road that passes the Yew Tree Inn, you could not fail to notice the old quarry workings. These are called Leicester Mill Quarries, but today the most prominent of them has been named Anglezarke quarry by climbers, with whom it is very popular. It has one very famous climb called the Golden Tower. It is straight opposite and slightly to the right as you go in through either of the two gaps. It's very appropriately named, but you rarely see anyone climb it, it is so difficult. All these quarries produced stone setts for road making between 1880 and 1920. There are more climbs in the other quarry further along the bottom road that goes to High Bullough Reservoir. (Guidebook: Rock climbs in Lancashire and the North West—published by Cicerone Press).

If you want to look at Rivington village and the Hall Barn on this walk, see the notes to Walk No. 1.4.

* Equally well from this point you can go round the Yarrow Res. To do this keep straight on past Deane House Cottage where there is a stile into the field. The path is fairly well trodden and way marked with yellow plastic arrows right to a stile onto the road. Turn left here and go down it until you come to the start of a stony cart track on the left. It runs round the lower edge of the reservoir and takes you easily back to Rivington opposite the School.

THE ROUND OF HEALEY NAB, WATERMANS COTTAGE, AND WHITE COPPICE WALK NO. **1.10**

The best place to start is Thomas Witter's works at Heapey. You climb the Nab first and then you can decide whether to go on or return by a shorter route to your car.

Time required: About 2 hours, but all of that could be spent wandering around the Nab. One hour is sufficient for a shorter walk just to go up the Nab and back.

To find the works, take the A674 out of Chorley, and turn right immediately this road has crossed the M61. The works lie a mile ahead. Parking off the road can just be managed. Turn back along the road for a couple of hundred yards to the start of a cindered cart track on the left. It passes a cottage and skirts the works fence, then joins another track coming down the hill. Turn left, on this track and follow it easily until it reaches the road. The views are highly contrasted: on the left the squalor of a paper mill, on the right the pastures crowned by the woods of the Nab.

At the road corner take the cart track leading to Higher Healey Farm. Skirt the farm on the right, then take the cart track that runs between a hedge and a fence into the woods. Soon after entering them there is a stile on the left. This is where you go to the top of the Nab. There are good views of White Coppice and Great Hill. Return to the cart track by an obvious path that starts at the entrance of the quarry. The stile opposite is the start of a footpath that runs down through the fields to the cindered cart track you started on. Turn right, where the cart track swings left, keep straight on along a little grass track which leads to another cinder track and so back to your car. It will take you about 35 minutes from the top.

Let's continue on the main cart track through the woods. After leaving the woods the path is extremely wide and fenced on both sides. After about ¼ mile a pair of stiles allow another path to cross the one you are on. Use the left hand stile and follow the fence through a couple of fields. The path is not well marked at first, it improves, then disappears in a peaty area that was the site of a big fire in 1976. It reappears at the next wall, and then is unmistakable down to the road near the Waterman's Cottage, a picturesque mock Tudor building belonging originally to Liverpool Corporation Water Works. Turn right on the road which goes round the head of the Anglezarke Reservoir and just past the cottage you will see a swing gate on the left and a path going sharp left to White Coppice. This is the same path as used in Walk No. 1.6. This

The Waterman's Cottage

time cross the bridge over the Goit, and immediately turn right. The path is faint, especially in winter, but keep to the wall side and you will find stiles in the next two fences. After that aim left a bit, passing between a pair of old oak trees, and you will see a gate that leads to a cart track that goes directly to the farm yard of White Coppice Farm. As soon as you reach the tarmac road, turn left and left again in about 100 yards. At the junction by the bridge take the right hand fork, and almost at once cross the stream by a foot bridge and follow the path along the bank of the reservoirs back to Witter's Mill. When you reach the huge pipe, go past it on the right and at the next gate, usually locked, go through the stile on the right. Then drop left below the reservoir and in a few yards you will find yourself on the road by the works, almost within sight of your car.

Things of interest
Higher Healey Farm is a Grade 2 listed building whose date stone is almost illegible. It has been extended quite recently in a completely harmonious manner in contrast with some alterations in very poor taste that have been done in the Area.

The Nab top quarry was worked up to about 1920, but there are much older ones and some old bell pits where coal was mined perhaps 200 years ago on the side facing the Waterman's Cottage, above the cart track.

If you do this walk in June when the wild flowers are at their best, you will find the stream from White Coppice to the small reservoirs above Witter's mill has a good selection, particularly of the Umbelliferae family. These are the plants with a lot of small white flowers arranged like a flattish umbrella — hence the Latin name. By the stream that runs between the old cottages and the road you will see ground elder, wild angelica, and cow parsley all growing close together. The umbelliferae are not spectacular flowers. There's a lot of similar ones and it does help to see them close together if you're interested in identifying them, which is not easy and depends more on leaf and seed shape than the actual flowers. Other common ones of the family are: hogweed — large and coarse as its name suggests; sweet cicely, which closely resembles cow parsley but smells of aniseed, and the earth nut, a smaller wiry leaved plant growing in many of the fields on the Nab.

After crossing the footbridge a surprising find on the stream side is watercress, with a white flower like candytuft in June. Lower down, just before the first reservoir, there's some brooklime, a bright blue flower, rather like forget-me-not, but brighter and with only 4 petals not 5. There's the occasional yellow flag iris, too, and pink bistort completes a fine colour scheme. The banks of the last reservoir have an interesting selection in August — marsh woundwort, common skull cap, greater willow herb — as well as the more common rosebay willow herb, water mint, and in the water itself, the common burr reed. There is hemlock water dropwort, a most poisonous plant, on the bank of the upper reservoir. On the very last bit of track down to the road there's a different selection — a big patch of greater stitchwort, red campion, goosegrass, tufted vetch, as well as willow herb and a good collection of nettles and brambles.

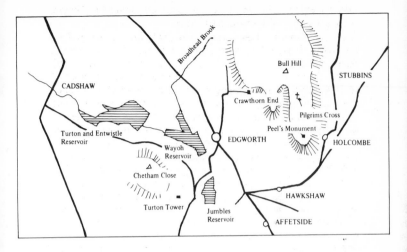

2. WALKS AROUND BOLTON AND BURY

WALKS ROUND WAYOH RESERVOIR AND TURTON AND ENTWISTLE RESERVOIR.   WALK NO. 2.1

The North West Water Authority now manages these reservoirs, but there are many notices of Bolton Corporation Water Works still in place.

1. Walking round Wayoh Reservoir

Park at either end of the dam across the reservoir. To find it, take the minor road that leaves the A676 just north of Edgworth at Hob Lane Farm. There are buses to Edgworth and some trains stop at Edgworth station, which makes quite a good starting place for this walk.

The dam divides the reservoirs into two and the walk round may be split here if you wish. It is suitable for shoes and any weather, and can be done either way round equally well. Time: about 1½ hours.

The start of the cart track running south along the Edgworth side of the reservoir is obvious, as indeed is the track all the way to the lower dam. Cross this lower dam and you will find the track again where the wall finishes, this time a more pleasing footpath. It crosses the narrow western arm of the reservoir on a little causeway from which you get a very impressive view of the railway line, high on a set of arches, crossing the reservoir a little higher up. Turn right as soon as you reach the 'mainland' and follow the track round the edge until it climbs up very steeply for the last few yards to a farm road. The macadam road is now only a few yards away and 5 minutes will see you back to your car if you wish. Assuming you want to continue round the rest, which is the best part anyway, cross the road and find the start of the path in the woods. The path runs plainly all the way round crossing two little streams on good bridges.

2. Walking round Turton and Entwistle Reservoir

The best approach is by the lane that leaves the B6391 about ½ mile on the western side of the railway line. It is signposted for Entwistle but is only tarmac as far as the dam. After that it is extremely rough. Park by the embankment as soon as you come to it.

Time: about 1 hour. Suitable for shoes and any weather.

Start at the gate in the embankment wall near where you are parked. This path along the south side quickly establishes the character of the reservoir as a moorland one, quite different from the Wayoh. Turton Moor at the head is framed by steep

Wayoh Reservoir

tree-lined valley sides. The path all the way is straight-forward and unmistakable. It crosses the inflow stream by a narrow bridge and a stile brings you back to the water's edge on the other side of the stream. Later the path leaves the water's edge to join a cinder track. This brings you back to the dam on the other side of which you are parked.

Things of interest seen on these two walks
The upper arm of Wayoh reservoir gives a sheltered spot for many of the commoner flowers that can be found in the Area. Amongst them you may find:

In Spring; celandine, hundreds of them; marsh marigolds; butterburr; daises; flowering currant, a garden escape; common scurvey grass — not a grass and not so common; bluebells; buttercups; ladies mantle; dandelion; horses tail — an unusual sort of plant, a bit like a branch off a pine tree with a sort of cone for a flower.

In Summer: meadow sweet; rosebay willow herb; bistort; blackberry; wild raspberry; common comfrey.

In contrast, the Turton and Entwistle Reservoir, being moorland in character and lined with Scots fir plantations, does not have a very varied collection of flowers. Heather and bilberries are common.

There is a good schematic map at the dam on this latter reservoir that will help you sort out the geography of the place. If you are interested in old buildings it is worth a small diversion to have a look at Entwistle Hall, which is in the lane of that name. It is a fine stone built place, characteristic of the best of the old farm buildings in the 'Bolton Uplands'. It is a Grade 2 listed building.

You may see duck, coots, jack snipe and other water birds on these reservoirs. In the woods around Turton and Entwistle Reservoir there are robins, wrens, cole, blue and great tits, linnets, jays, and magpies.

*Holcombe Hill with Peel's Monument
behind the Turton and Entwistle Reservoir*

TWO WALKS ROUND CADSHAW (YARNSDALE)

Both these walks start at the same point on the A666 road which divides the valley into an upper and lower part. To find a place to park if you are approaching from the Bolton side, look for the minor road that leaves it just on the north side of the Charters Moss Plantation, turn to the right down this and park in a lay-bye.

Cadshaw Valley

First let's look at the lower valley. It takes 30-40 minutes and is suitable for shoes. The path starts on the main road just beyond the junction at a stile by a clump of trees. It is marked by a sign post for Egerton. Follow the broad track round the hillside to Cadshaw Quarry. Cadshaw Rocks (Fairy Rocks) can be seen across the delightful little vale. They are popular with rock climbers and can be reached from the quarry by a slight path which crosses the stream. Return as you came.

The track or the walk in the upper part of the valley starts about 100 yards further up the road. The gateway is marked with finger post to Belmont. The cart track climbs gently up the side of the valley, passing a pond on the right where water crowfoot grows. There are one or two side tracks but ignore these until you come to one marked by the remains of a tall finger post. Take the right hand one: the left hand one ends at some old coal pits just up the valley. Your track quickly

73

becomes a thready little thing. Follow it carefully to the stream where there is a bridge. You need that bridge to cross the stream because right down this valley it is enclosed in vertical stone walls that make crossing very difficult indeed. Once you're across, climb steeply up to the cart track and turn right. If you turn left, you go either to Darwen or Belmont. Follow the cart track to a gate but do not go through it. Instead, take another thready little track through green pastures aiming at a clump of trees by the fence. There you will find a stile to a cart track which will lead you back to the road. Your car is out of sight, about ¼ mile away.

Things of interest

The view down the reservoir soon after you start the first walk is very fine. Holcombe Hill with Peel's Monument is straight ahead.

Cadshaw Rocks is a small natural gritstone cliff, not in any way quarried, but formed by faulting and earth slips. It offers a very good selection of climbs and most summer evenings climbers can be seen in action there.

The cart tracks up the valley on the second walk were once used to bring coal from the mines on the moors. They are quite well supplied with springs and wells where today you will see water crowfoot growing. It flowers in early summer and must have shallow water to grow. It is no relation of the water cress and is not edible. One of the old wells on the return track is heavily stained with ochre, a sign of underground iron deposits.

A WALK FROM JUMBLES RESERVOIR ROUND AFFETSIDE, HAWKSHAW, AND TURTON BOTTOMS
WALK NO. **2.3**

This would be a splendid circular walk through pastures, woods, and by streams if only the footpath between Hawkshaw and Quarlton Fold had not disappeared. This means you now have to do a good mile along the road from Hawkshaw to the end of Walves Reservoir to find a path down to Turton Bottoms. But it's worth it. Alternatively you can divide this walk into two short ones, each returning as you came, but this is never so satisfying as a round tour.

Time for the circuit: 2½-3 hours.

Park at the improved Water Fold car park on Jumbles Res. If you are coming from Bolton on the A676 turn left down a lane just after two detached brick houses on the right. If you are coming from Blackburn take the first turn on the right after the Lamb Inn. There are only very small signs for Jumbles Reservoir at the end of this lane.

Leave the car park by the corner nearest the reservoir to find a little footpath that runs by the fence down to the old lane that starts at Bromley Cross station, crosses Bradshaw Brook and then goes on to join the A676. Turn left when you get to this lane, follow it to the road, cross the road and go up the lane opposite. This has been given new metal stiles and gates and leads to the Water Authority's treatment plant. The right of way has been diverted round the right hand side, and isn't very clear. However, when you've passed the new metal fence slant leftwards to the wall where you will pick up the old track again. It continues between two walls for a little way, then gets a bit difficult to follow when the walls end. Keep in the same general direction and you'll find it again by the next wall and that will lead you straight to Affetside. Turn left on the road if you want to look at the Headless Cross, one of the Ancient Monuments of the Area. It's about 50 yards down the road.

The Pack Horse Inn is almost straight opposite you when you come to the road, and the path you want goes down by the side of it. Turn right when you reach the road, cross it, and almost at once turn left down a footpath marked by a finger post. This takes you most pleasantly through hay fields, by the side of a small reservoir. When you have passed the reservoir the path is faint for a little while. Bear left, going quite steeply downhill and it soon becomes very good again, bringing you on to a cart track. Turn right here and then take the left fork and you will be in Hawkshaw in another 5 minutes.

Turn left on the main road in Hawkshaw and stay on this road to the cross roads at the Bull where you turn right along the Edgworth road. Keep going until just after you have passed the Walves Reservoir and you see a cart track marked 'footpath' on the left. Make sure you take the correct one, not the concreted lane that leads to Birches Farm that starts only 50 yards away. There's no pleasure in walking this latter, whereas the correct lane is hedged with hawthorn and wild roses, shaded with tall trees, and full of summer flowers. It brings you into Turton Bottoms by the side of Quarlton Vale Bleach Works, ruined and no longer used. Turn left here, bear left at the next fork and right into Birches Road. Cross the stream at the end of the cottages, keep left, and cross the second stream by the old pack horse bridge. Turn left when you meet the rough road and follow it into a factory yard. Keep to the right hand edge of this and you will soon find the riverside path that leads you through to the Jumbles Reservoir. Follow any of the many variations of path that exist until you come to the reservoir side, where a cart track will see you back to your car.

From Hawkshaw to Affetside
This is one of the best bits of the previous walk if you don't want to do the whole lot. It will take about 1¼ hours return, and is best done from Hawkshaw on the Bolton-Burnley road between Bradshaw and Ramsbottom. Park in Hawkshaw Lane between the P.O. and the pub.

Cross the main road and go down a rough cart track straight opposite. Follow this, forking right, until it crosses the outflow over a weir from a small reservoir. On the left, rather inconspicuous, there is a swing gate into a field. The footpath is faint at first, but rapidly improves and becomes a good track contouring the little valley almost to Two Brooks Farm. Then it climbs steeply, goes between two small reservoirs and up through hayfields to the B6213 Tottington road. Cross this road and 50 yards away on the right, another footpath starts and will lead you up by the side of the Pack Horse at Affetside. It seems as if this path only goes to a stylishly re-built farm, but it goes right in front of it and then on by the left hand corner. Return as you came.

From Jumbles Reservoir to Turton Bottoms

This is the other good bit of the long one, but it is even better if you start at Bromley Cross station where there is parking space and return there by bus from the Spread Eagle at Turton. These instructions are for that walk. (If you prefer to start at Jumbles Reservoir, see page No. 00 for details on how to find the car park there, and start walking from that point, indicated * below) To find Bromley Cross station, take the B6391, which is a minor road leaving the A676 Bolton-Burnley road at Bradshaw and running to meet the A666 Bolton-Darwen road.

Time: about 1½ hours

Cross the railway line by the level crossing, turn right and almost at once turn left on to an unmade road. Soon after you've passed the last house on the left, a path goes off into the field on the right. Follow this down into the valley and cross Bradshaw Brook by a white metal bridge. Climb up a little and you will see a quarry straight ahead with a fence running up to it on the left. There is a purpose-made gap in this fence and from here a path leads to the car park at Jumbles Reservoir. * From the car park a cart track runs round the edge of the reservoir to the bridge that crosses the narrow end. You don't use this, keep straight ahead on the footpath that leads into the little gorge of Turton Bottoms. Just follow the path which lies near the brook all the time and comes out in a works yard in the Bottoms. Here you keep left, cross the stream and a hundred yards further on take a cinder track to the right. It crosses the old pack saddle bridge, then another one, and winds its way amongst the old cottages of the Bottoms. Any left turn will bring you to the main road close to the Spread Eagle and the bus stop.

Things of interest seen on these last three walks.

Jumbles reservoir is not used as a source of domestic water as are the others above it, but is used to store compensation water for release into Bradshaw Brook as required. The road at Affetside is built on the site of the Roman road that ran from Manchester to Ribchester, but nothing remains of it. The Headless Cross is listed as an Ancient Monument, and the pub, the Pack Horse, is a listed building.

Going down to Hawkshaw, the little reservoir is fringed with forget-me-nots in June and often has great flotillas of tadpoles. A little below it, you will see an isolated chimney on the hillside and perhaps wonder where the mill was situated. The mill was right down on the valley bottom and has been demolished. In the early years of the last century the processing of cotton cloth was done out-of-doors, allowing the sun and the rain to do the work that is now done by chemicals. When steam power came along, soot from the chimney spoiled the cloth, so new chimneys were built high on the hillside to take the soots away. They were connected to the mill boilers by a long complex system of flues, which increased the overall height and therefore the draught.

The lane from Walves reservoir leaves the road at a spot known as Bottom o' Knotts Brow, the site of the old Roman road, Watling Steet. The spot is listed as an Ancient Monument. This lane is full of summer flowers including harebell and ladies mantle, neither of them common in the Area.

Turton Bottoms itself is a Conservation Area and is described more fully elsewhere in this book. Soon after you start going down the woods you will see an old water leat, at one time connected to the water wheel which now stands at Turton Tower awaiting restoration. Near the end of the leat there is a dripping wet sandstone outcrop. It is crowned with tufts of hairy woodrush, and besides supporting a large and varied growth of mosses, has a patch of golden saxifrage, another not-so-common plant. In the woods themselves butterburr grows everywhere. In early Spring it throws a bold if dull flower head before the rhubarb-like leaves arrive and cover everything. Besides that, there is a good selection of moisture loving plants — bistort, sweet cicely, rosebay willow herb, honeysuckle.

At the northern end of the reservoir quarrying has laid bare a section of the ground revealing the underlaying rock strata. At the bottom is a massive layer of fine-grained sandstone topped by many layers of shale, bearing traces of coal. On top of this there is a layer of boulder clay, left by the last glacial epoque, some 8-9 thousand years ago. Topmost of all is a thin layer of soil, indicative of the relatively low fertility of the Area.

FROM HAWKSHAW TO BULL HILL AND PEEL'S MONUMENT

WALK NO. **2.4**

Starting at Hawkshaw this makes a very fine afternoons walk, but as it goes through the Army's Firing Range, is subject to the same access problem as Walk No. 3.1 so read those notes. The Army has also closed many of the footpaths that could be used to return to Hawkshaw.

Parking at Hawkshaw, which is on the A676 Burnley-Bolton road, is difficult, but can be managed in Hawkshaw Lane between the post office and the pub. This is where the walk starts.

Time: about 4 hours.

Follow the lane right up the hill passing a number of attractive stone farms some of which are listed buildings. When you come to the T junction, turn left to Graining Farm. Follow the cart track sharply round the corner of the building and almost at once you will see a swing gate on your left. Go through this and the next one, cross the tiny stream and then at once turn right and follow the stream up the hill. The path has virtually disappeared, but make diagonally left over the rough pastures aiming at a group of buildings on the cart track that runs

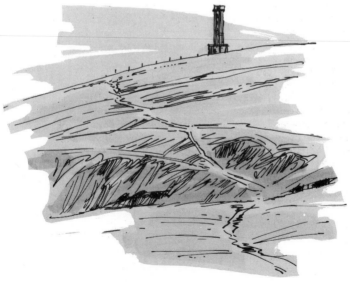

Peel's Monument from Harcles Hill

79

around the edge of the moor. When you've reached this cart track by the buildings, turn left, and as soon as you've crossed the biggish stream that runs under the road, as it is here, strike steeply up right aiming below the fence of another set of buildings in order to meet the track from Crowthorn End Farm that goes up Bull Hill. Just below these buildings turn left on an old paved track. It only lasts a few yards, ending at a gateway. Go through the gateway, turn right and follow the wall. The track is scarcely visible here, but at the end of the wall becomes well marked if very boggy. It leads direct to the top of Bull Hill. The views from Bull Hill are very fine indeed if it is clear. See Walk No. 3.1 for an indication of what you may see.

From Bull Hill move off roughly south east, that's to say, towards Bury. There's no path, but it's not bad going. Soon you will see the Stone on the Site of the Pilgrim's Cross, and after that you will find a good path which winds its way between the two summits of Harcles Hill. You, however, are a purist, putting in all the summits, so make a little diversion to do this. From the top of the second one Peel's Monument can be seen clearly, and a reasonable track will lead you to it. From the monument a broad track leads on over the brow of the hill, passes a farm at a zig-zag and drops down to a bridleway that runs right round Holcombe Head to Crowthorn Reservoir. It once served a whole line of upland farms, now mostly empty and ruined.

When Bank Top Farm comes into view, keep a sharp look out for a low stone stile on your left. It's right by an especially large stone gate post, and on the other side of the track, there's a gnarled hawthorn. Go over the stile and follow a line of them right down into the wooded valley of Hawkshaw Brook. Where a barbed wire fence has been put across the path, turn right—it's rather easier going and will bring you to the same place: the skeleton remains of a one-time substantial bridge. If your balance is good and you've a head for heights, be bold and walk across one of the iron girders. Otherwise paddle or make a dash for it through the water! Cross the stile and turn left up to Redisher Farm. Go straight ahead down the lane to the main road, unfortunately a good mile from your car.

Things of interest

Hawkshaw Lane, at first metalled, then becoming rough and giving agreeable walking, crosses the pastures leading up to the moors, and on it stand a number of fine old farm houses. In places it runs between bankings crowned with wild rose and hawthorn, and gives good views of the central moors of the Area.

Just before you come to Lower Graining Farm there is a tiny cemetery on your left. It contains just one tombstone, or rather, two for the same grave: the original one now cracked and repaired and cracked again, and a modern one side by side. This modern one tells just a little of the story. Roger Worthington was a Baptist minister who died in 1709 aged about 50. He doesn't seem to have been attached to a church, but to have been something of a hermit or a travelling preacher, going amongst the moorland folk who were strong non-conformists, preaching to them. Certainly he must have had a great love of these moors to have been buried alone at the foot of them. See Walk No. 3.2 for a note about the Stone on the Site of the Pilgrim's Cross.

A WALK OVER CHETHAM CLOSE, TURTON.

WALK NO. **2.5**

This walk starts at the car park at Turton Tower, which lies just off the B6391 a few hundred yards south of Chapeltown. Time: about 1½-2 hours.

From the car park a pleasant footpath takes you through the woods into a coke storage yard by the railway. Press on — it is a footpath. Cross the railway by the level crossing and bear left into the stile in the corner by the house. The path leads up the field, crosses a cart track and shortly aferwards disappears. Don't worry, just aim at the trees, and you will find the track again after it has passed through all that's left of a fence and gate. Follow it until you come to a fence, go over the stile, turn right and follow the fence until the ground starts to level out. Then keep your eyes open for a little track that goes off to the left direct to the ordnance survey cairn on top. Chetham Close is 329 metres high, (1080 ft.) It is not quite as high as Turton Heights, (335 metres or 1100 ft.) A few yards away to the right are the remains of two stone circles. Very little indeed remains, but they're worth a look. (To visit Turton Heights follow the crest of the moor. Easy going. Return same way. Adds about 30 mins. to the walk.)

The Railway Bridge

Continue following the path across the first wall to a white painted iron stump. Here you join a path that comes up from Egerton. Turn right, and follow it for a few minutes until it starts to swing left. Instead, keep straight on. There's a bit of path to follow. Go through a gap in the wall and aim at the long wall running downhill on your right. There's a stile in the fence at the bottom that brings you on to the metalled road leading to Clough House Farm. Follow it past the farm and past the track leading up from the mill that you used to start the walk. Then when this cart track goes through a gate to join another cart track, turn left, and a few more minutes brings you back over the railway to Turton Towers. This railway bridge is an interesting architectural curiosity, built in the style of a Norman castle.

WAYOH AND THE BROADHEAD VALLEY

This walk covers some very varied countryside along the upper part of the Wayoh Reservoir and up the north-east side of the Broadhead Valley to Lower House. The first part of the return across the valley to the farm (Orrell Cote, not named on the map) below Stanley Hill is not easy to follow, and this return is only recommended if you are experienced in following disused footpaths.

Time: 2½ hrs. or 1½ hrs. if you return as you came.

Turn off the A676 Bolton-Burnley road at Walves Reservoir to get to Edgworth, then take the Blackburn road. Turn left at Hob Lane Farm and park down by the reservoir embankment. Alternatively, and possibly better, park in the start of School Lane, almost opposite Hob Lane.

Walk down Hob Lane to the reservoir, and go along the path that goes round its northern arm. It doesn't matter which side you take. If you've chosen the near side, cross Broadhead Brook and then Wayoh Brook and almost immediately turn right. If you prefer the other side turn left before you've crossed Wayoh Brook. Go over a stile and up to a pond then descend to the brook and cross it on a footbridge. Now follow this path up to Wayoh Fold Farm. As you approach the farm make for the gate to the left of the buildings and go straight ahead on the farm track, past a barn of unusual design, onto the road. Turn left up the road, and about 50 yards away you will see a footpath sign post. Take this track up to Naze End, staying on the lower one when it forks. (At the last building of this ruined farm make a diversion left if you are interested in industrial archaeology. Go up by the wall, cross it at the first wall junction and go diagonally right for less than 100 yards. There you will find the remains of seven beehive type coke ovens. They are most unusual.)

If you do not feel able to do your bit towards opening up the disused paths, then go back towards a pair of stumps on the moor and from there to a gate (beware of an electric fence, for this is not a right of way). Straight ahead will now bring you above the footpath where you started. Drop down onto this and return to your car either along the road which is not unpleasant, or retrace your steps by the reservoir.

If you boldly decide to do your bit, regain the cart track up the valley to the next farm, Lower House, also deserted. Here, at the end of the buildings there is a stile in the trees and a path goes down the field to a stile to the river. The bridge has completely gone, but you won't find any difficulty in crossing a few yards above it. Now the difficulties start. Follow the little side-stream until you come to a collapsed bridge. Cross the stream — it's easy enough just above the bridge. Then climb steeply through a tangle of vegetation for about 50 yards. It soon becomes much easier. Follow the stream and the path improves all the way to Hall Hill Farm, yet another deserted farm. Here the path is between walls and goes sharply left up to another farm by the road. You leave it here and go slightly right into the field. The path is barely visible, but follow the wall closely down the field to the stream that runs in a steep gully. Again the bridge is collapsed but again it is easy to cross just below it. There's still no path. The right of way goes on the right hand side of the fence, but it is not possible to get into the farm yard here. It is better to go left over the stile as soon as you've crossed the river and then go up to the farm on that side. You will find a stile opposite the farm building that brings you on to the cart track leading to them. Follow this cart track back to the road. Turn right and then left in about 50 yards to Moorside Farm. Go left between the farm and the barn to find the stile into the field and follow this path to Hill Top Farm. Go through the elegant forecourt of the house through the side gate onto the lane. Follow the lane turning right at the junction just above the school, and continue down the road to your car.

Things of interest
The banks of the upper arm of the Wayoh Reservoir support a good selection of wild flowers. See Walk No. 2.1 for a list of some of them. The Broadhead Valley's name describes its appearance exactly. When you have crossed the valley to Orrell Cote Farm, look back and you will see that the moorland on the side of the valley you have just left extends considerably lower down the sides of the valley than on the side where you are now walking. The reason for this is that it faces the prevailing wind and gets a heavier rainfall, and when this exceeds about 50-60 inches per annum, moorland overtakes pasture. The things of greatest interest in this walk are the beehive coke ovens above Naze end. They are of the earliest type and it is possible that they were built as long ago as 1800. Coal was mined on the spot as well as a little higher up the valley. There are still fragments of coal and coke around.

FROM HORROCKS FOLD TO BELMONT BY
LONGWORTH CLOUGH   WALK NO. 2.7

The start of this walk isn't really up to standard, but the finishing part is excellent. In many ways it would be just as well to start near Higher Critchley Fold, but how do you get back there from Belmont except rather drearily along the road? At least by starting at Horrocks Fold you can come back on the bus. They are rather infrequent, so ring Bolton 32131 for their times and allow 2½ hours for the walk. (If you decide to start near Higher Critchley Fold, take the Belmont road from Egerton. The cinder track starts as soon as the road has crossed the brook and joins the main walk at the bridge over Eagley Brook.)

Starting from Horrocks Fold, take the A675 out of Bolton, until soon after passing Sweetloves Reservoir, houses on the right come to an abrupt end. Turn right at the end of them and park. Go straight on and continue on to the gravel track past the works to a house and then by a field path to one of the dozens of small mill reservoirs in this part of Bolton. From the corner of the reservoir cut across by a tip to a cinder track to the right. Follow this to its first fork, turn left, and keep left when another cinder track comes in from the right. You now join a bit of tarmac but not for long. It goes up the hill to the golf club, you go right, along a wide cinder track. It's walled, thick with blackberry, and divides Dunscar golf course into two. Then it descends gently to Eagley Brook. Cross the bridge and go straight on up the brookside, rich with flowers in Spring and Summer, to the paper mill.

The way through the mill buildings is as follows: As you enter the complex, follow the tarmac until it turns sharp left. There keep straight on, up a bit of old cobbled path and some steps to a storage area slightly on your right. Go through this area, and when the road forks, take the right hand branch which will take you out of the mill area and on to a farm. Immediately past the farm there is a swing gate on the right. Go through this. The track is faint, but aim at the water leat ahead where it is good. Follow the leat right round the curve of Longworth Clough, whose woods and stream can be well seen from this high level and unusual path. Where it meets the dam of the Ornamental Reservoir turn right across the dam, go over the bridge and straight up the field to a stile to the road in the corner by a tree. This is often a hayfield and the track barely visible. Keep in single file. If you are walking back to Higher Critchley Fold, turn right here . Otherwise turn left and follow the road down to the works of the Belmont Dyeing and Bleaching Co. Take a short cut by their visitors' car park direct to Maria Square and the bus stop, Belmont. You should have time for a look around this spot.

Things of interest

Longworth Clough is famous for its flowers, and there are several sites of special interest to botanists. In the marshy woods below the paper mill you can see marsh marigolds, mayflowers, bistort, Himalayan balsam, meadow sweet, and one fairly rare one — pink purselane.

The water leat is another good place for moisture loving plants. There you may find the common valerian, not so common round here. Towards its end the leat is becoming choked with plants and reeds. This is really pond sedge. There's a much better known sedge in the Ornamental Reservoir, — the bulrush. The woods in the upper part of the clough contain many rowans and are carpeted with bilberry in places.

Belmont Village has one of the finest situations in the whole of the Area. Whilst not a moorland village, it is much influenced by them. You will find the best views of it from the east, around Higher Whittacker, for example. There are a number of listed buildings in the main street of which Maria Square, built in 1804, is perhaps the best example. On the opposite corner from its distinctive name plate is an old 'Sabbath School' built in 1832. Originally in cut stone like the rest of the square, it has been heavily rendered at some time, losing character. A further item of interest in this corner is the granite obelisk commemorating the struggle that the residents of Belmont had to gain 'rights for all time and to perpetuity' of compensation water from the Belmont reservoir when it was taken over by Bolton Corporation in 1907. It was quite an affair judging by the inscription. Across the road, opposite the Black Dog, is one of the many drinking fountains and troughs erected to celebrate Queen Victoria's Diamond Jubilee. Today the water no longer flows and the trough is planted with flowers.

BARROW BRIDGE, DEAN BROOK, AND RIVINGTON PIKE

WALK NO. **2.8**

Barrow Bridge is a beauty spot known to the people of Bolton for many years. It used to have a tea-room; today it has a car-park and picnic place and is a Conservation Area. The walk to the Pike is quite long but the walk up Dean Brook only takes an hour there and back.

It's best to get to Barrow Bridge by leaving the Moss Bank Way ring road, A58, at Moss Bank Park and generally keeping left until you come to the end of the road at Barrow Bridge. There's also a bus service from Bolton.

Dean Brook and Barrow Bridge

The short walk

Go on up the road passing the car park in a few hundred yards. There are some fine old houses both at the road side and across the water leat, a feature of the place. Continue the length of the road until it turns sharp right, uphill. At the end is a path leading to a set of steps, at the foot of which, on the right, is a stile. This is the start of the footpath up Dean Brook, a delightful wooded clough. After the first bridge the brook is quite large and difficult to cross in a wet spell. If this is the case, walk along it and just as the hillside gets too steep to manage, you will find four good stepping stones to get you back. Then there's no need to cross again until the very end, just before you reach the road at Walker Fold Farm. Then it's easy.

Here, if time is short, go left up the hill to the farm where there is a footpath marked by a finger post that leads quickly and directly back to Barrow Bridge. If you have a little more time you may prefer to turn right up the road, go past Colliers Row to the lane opposite the old School. Turn down this and you will be back in Barrow Bridge within 10 or 15 minutes.

The long walk

If you have a whole afternoon to spare this extends the previous walk to include some good moorland walking and some of the best views in the Area — if it's clear. In fact, it's one of the best walks. It is easier to use public transport: bus to Barrow Bridge from Bolton, and bus back to Bolton from Horwich.

Go to Walker Fold Farm as just described. Turn left on the road and just past the farm a finger post directs you to the required footpath on the right. It may be very wet to start, but eventually improves with a row of paving stones down the middle. It ends at the former Burnt Edge Colliery, and a few yards higher up the hillside another track comes slanting in from the left. Go up to it, and follow it up the rest of the valley. At the valley head it curves gently right and crosses a little stream. Within 50 or 60 yards a wall comes in on the left and a path branches off and runs up besides it. Follow this track until it reaches the metalled road leading to the T.V. mast on Winter Hill. (From here it is possible to reverse route 1.14). Turn right and after about 100 yards a track leads off on the left, passes a water intake, and goes down to the upper part of Georges Lane. (If you want to go up Winter Hill as well, keep on the metalled road all the way. See Walk No. 1.5 for some guidance). Follow Georges Lane to the foot of the Pike, climb it and enjoy the views. The quickest way back to Horwich is to return down Georges Lane to a big clump of rhododendrons. Just before you get there, there is a swing gate on the right leading to a grassy cart track that runs down to Higher Knoll Farm. From there it's concreted, and takes you down to the rough lane behind Rivington School. Turn left and left again onto Lever Park Avenue, and you will find the bus stop at the end of it by the main road.

Whilst you are on the Pike you are very close to the Ornamental Gardens. Have a look there if you've time. The rough road that divides them in two will take you down to the Rivington School. Allow about half an hour to the bus stop. See the 'Things of interest' section for walks in Section One for a description of the Pike, the Ornamental Gardens and Lever Park.

Things of interest
Dean Brook Wood is typical of the wooded cloughs on the western edge of the moors. It is mainly oak with some birch, sycamore, and alder by the brook and is carpeted with bluebells in the spring. Across the top the upper part has been planted with spruce and beech, and is not really in character. Colliers Row originally housed the colliers who worked at the former Burnt Edge Colliery about a mile further up the brook. The school further along Scout Road was built to educate their children. It is now a Grade 2 listed building. Behind Colliers Row is Brownstones quarry, much used by local climbers as a practice ground. It was one of the first quarries in Britain to be used for climbing.

A WALK AROUND AINSWORTH   WALK NO. 2.9

This is a pleasant walk round the pastures and reservoirs behind Ainsworth, which sits astride the B6196 Bury-Bradshaw road. Park in any convenient side street near the Co-op.

Time: About ¾ hour.

First have a look round the Parish Church and then start up Knowsley Street which is opposite. You pass the Unitarian Chapel on your left and just after it, a small but fine old cottage. Continue up the road which soon becomes a lane. Turn right at the first 'cross roads', passing a row of beautiful ivy covered cottages on you left. The next section of path is liable to be muddy, but it's short. When you come to the lane, turn left, and in about 50 yards you will see a stile on the right leading to the reservoir. Cross its embankment and where the track forks in three directions take the left hand one, making for the end of a wall. You will find a stile behind it leading you into the lane that goes up to Meadow Croft Farm.

Do not go into the farm yard, but keep straight on along a grassy lane. The path disappears now, but keep to the hedge side and cut down to the bridge across the reservoir only when you're almost opposite it. Turn left and climb up by the hedge side. When you're almost in sight of the hospital you have a choice of ways. Either keep straight on past it until you re-join your starting track close to the row of ivy covered cottages, or, make a slight extension to look at Barrack Fold Farm.

To do this, turn right through the meadow when you reach a hedge coming in on your left. The path is reasonable well marked, but it needs a bit of care to start it correctly. Then a line of stiles takes you right down past the back of the barn into the farm lane. Turn left and then right before you go into the farm yard—except, of course, to have a look at the house. This lane will take you back to Ainsworth whose church tower you will now be able to see. Where the lane makes a right angle bend to the left keep straight on through the stile onto a footpath that brings you to the back of the pub. Turn right down the side of the Unitarian Chapel, and you will then emerge through the stage coach gateway from the pub yard.

Things of interest

See the notes on Ainsworth in the chapter on Conservation Areas. Barrack Fold Farm was built in 1631 and takes its name from the legend that Oliver Cromwell billetted his troops here prior to the Battle of Bolton. It is a Grade 2 building and the datestone is one of the oldest in the Area.

A WALK ROUND BROOK FOLD AND THE HEIGHT, HARWOOD, BOLTON. WALK NO. **2.10**

This is one of the best short pasture land walks in the Area, passing one or two fine old houses at Brook Fold and having very good views from Winter Hill to Kinder Scout. The paths in the fields have almost disappeared, but the stiles are all present and it is not difficult to follow.

Time: About ¾ hour, just right for a fine evening.

From the B6196, go up the road that passes Harwood Golf Course for about ½ mile. It is just possible to park off the road either at the start of the path by the finger post on the left, or about 100 yards lower down where the golfers' paths cross the road. As soon as you're in the field aim slightly right to a hawthorn tree where you will find the next stile. Aim slightly left to find the next one, then straight across, then diagonally right up the hill. The path becomes a wide track between fences and leads into the cart track that goes down to the road. Turn left on it, pass the farm, and where this cart track (Brooks Lane) makes a sharp turn left just past the farm, turn right through a gate onto a path that runs up towards some long disused quarries. Shortly the path forks. Take the right-hand one and keep to the wall. At the end of it you will find a stile into the field. Keep along the wall side until you can see the gate and then make directly for it, turn left on the lane and go up to and past the next farm, Asmus Farm. You will find a swing gate at the end of the farm yard. Turn right as soon as you're through it and you will see the next stile. Now follow the fence and hedge right along to the lane that leads to the Height. Don't go down to this farm, the stiles run along the wall. Go straight across the lane — there's a stile, and go down towards the little river valley until you can see a pair of stone gate posts. Make for these and you will find yourself on a green cart track that leads to the road about 100 yards from where you started.

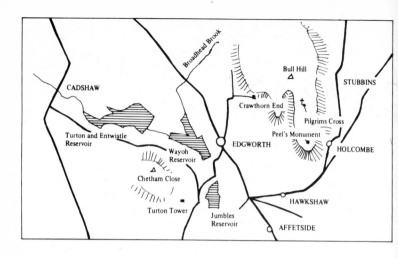

3. WALKS AROUND HELMSHORE, HASLINGDEN AND HOLCOMBE

Bull Hill and Harcles Hill

ASCENTS OF BULL HILL   WALK NO. **3.1**

As Bull Hill is the highest point (418 metres, 1372 ft.) in the eastern section of the Area, and is second only to Winter Hill (456 metres, 1498 ft.) in the whole Area its ascent deserves pride of place in this section. It is, however, somewhat bedevilled by the Army's firing ranges. Four danger areas are marked on the map and are liberally marked on the ground with notice boards stating, "Keep out when the red flag is flying." The flags can be seen from quite a distance away. Fortunately the Army do not use the ranges every day, especially in the winter, and the red flag is not flown often enough to prevent enjoyable walking round here. Ring Holcombe Moor Training Camp, Tottington 2876 or 2991 for the state of play.

The path from the B6214 Haslingden-Bury old road is the shortest way. It starts close to Buckden Wood, the only expanse of woodland on both sides of the road round here. Unfortunately it's not named on the map, though Lower Buckden Farm is and this gives you some guidance. There is a lay-by for parking on the west side of the road by the wood. Time: 30 min. to the top, 50 min. return, or two hours for the longer trip.

Take the cart track up the field marked by a sign post. At the next gate go straight ahead, fairly steeply to start, passing old mine spoil heaps on your right. It then runs more easily to the top of Bull Hill. Return as you came, or, if you prefer, extend the walk past the site of the Pilgrim's Cross and go down to Harcles Hill Farm by the track from there. At Harcles Hill Farm follow their road down the hill until it meets the cart track that runs all the way from near the White Horse, Helmshore, to Holcombe. Turn left on this track, not very clear in parts, until you come to Chatterton Close. Opposite the farm turn right down a lane that will bring you to the road and to your car in a couple of minutes.

93

If, however it is more convenient to start from the Bolton side of the hill, get to the road end above Crowthorn Reservoir by turning off the B6232 Blackburn-Haslingden road opposite the Grey Mare, following it to Crowthorn and then turning left, or from Bolton via Bradshaw and Edgworth.

Time: 50 min. return.

There is room to park off the road just past the white house of Crowthorn End. Then walk up the upper bit of tarmac road and just before it reaches the heavily fenced agricultural build-ings, turn left on an old paved track. It only lasts a few yards, ending at a gateway. Go through the gateway, turn right and follow the wall. The track is scarcely visible here, but at the end of the wall becomes well-marked if very boggy. It leads directly to the top of Bull Hill where a derisory red flag seems to fly permanently.

If you are using public transport, it is best to climb Bull Hill from Stubbins. Turn to Walk No. 3.4 to see how to start. When you reach the road after the first part of the wood, turn right and in about 100 yards you will see the finger post indicating the start of the walk just described.

A VISIT TO PEEL'S MONUMENT, HOLCOMBE

WALK NO. **3.2**

The monument stands stark on the skyline just above Holcombe. It was built in 1852 to celebrate the repeal of the Corn Laws, enacted between 1789 and 1815 to enforce the payment of a duty on imported corn. This made the price of bread artificially high — a far cry indeed from today's food subsidies. These laws caused grave hardship amongst the cotton operatives in Lancashire, and Sir Robert Peel, who was born in Bury in 1788, was Prime Minister of the government that repealed them.

For instructions for finding Holcombe and parking there, see Walk No. 3.3.

The shortest way for a quick visit will take you only about 30 min. return from the Shoulder Of Mutton at Holcombe, itself a delightful corner partly on a bridleway below the moor.

Across the road from the pub you will see a telephone kiosk. Turn left on the bridle-track here, turn right at the first junction, then left at the next one. The track zig-zags its way up in an obvious manner. Return as you came, or take small variations as the many tracks allow.

A much easier but longer way is to start as for the visit to the Pilgrim's Cross (No. 3.3) , but before reaching the quarries, turn left along the back of a wall. This track now runs more or less direct to the monument. If you wish to make the round trip, allow about 45 min.

VISIT TO THE SITE OF THE PILGRIM'S CROSS, HOLCOMBE
WALK NO. **3.3**

The site is on a very old track running between Bull Hill and Harcles Hill, but this track is now indistinct through lack of use and is difficult to find. Nowadays there is a good track from Harcles Hill Farm, though it is not a right of way.

To find Holcombe, get on to the B6214, the old Haslingden-Bury road. Holcombe is at the southern end, a short mile up the hill from Holcombe Brook. Parking is difficult. Just about the only place is the car park at the Shoulder of Mutton. If that's not possible, go down by the church and park below it. There's not much room there. Then walk back to the pub to start the walk.

Time: about 1½ hours.

From the pub cross the road and turn right. In 50 yards you will see the bridle track that runs parallel to the road. Follow it, climbing all the time, to the old school and the start of a cart track that goes up to the old quarries near Harcles Hill Farm. Follow this track until you are as high as the top wall of the farm enclosure. Cut across to the wall and go behind it past the farm buildings until you join the track coming up from the farm. Then follow this unmistakably to the site of the cross. Return by the same route, or if you have time continue to Peel's Monument. To do this, keep straight on at the farm. As soon as you're up the brow of the hill you will see the Monument.

The Pilgrim's Cross stood on one of the long lost tracks of Norman England. Its origins are lost in the mists of antiquity, and there seems to be no record of when it was placed there or when it was lost. However, there is a record that pilgrims travelling to Whalley Abbey rested and prayed there. The present stone was placed on the site on May 4th 1904, by the copyholders of the Manor of Holcombe and other interested people.

FROM STUBBINS ROUND BUCKDEN WOODS

Buckden Woods are National Trust property and make a delightful walk, but it is difficult to make a satisfactory round trip.

Stubbins is on the A56 between Ramsbottom and Rawtenstall. Park in a side street or at the Railway Hotel, which as its name suggests, is close to the railway bridge. Public transport will also get you there.

Time: 1-1¼ hours

From the Railway Hotel go under the railway and turn right. The road leads into Stubbins Vale Works, but it is also a footpath that leads right through. Follow it until it meets the railway, the old dismantled Helmshore line, but do not go under the bridge. Keep on the left hand side and the road soon becomes a cart track and the cart track a footpath that leads into the woods. At first there is only one way to go, but higher up the path forks. Take the right hand one, cross the brook by a huge stone slab — take care when it's wet — and re-cross about 70-80 yards higher up. This time there's no bridge, but it is not difficult. Now the path climbs on the left quite steeply and soon emerges on the road by a stile. You can cross the road and enter the upper part of the wood, also a National Trust property. The paths here are very thready and difficult to follow up the steep watercourse, and it's not nearly so enjoyable as the lower part. Eventually you can scramble out by a gate at the top close to where the footpath leads from the road to Bull Hill. Descend to the road by that path.

Go straight across the road down the lane that leads to Lower Buckden Farm. Very soon you will come to a branch on the right that passes a barn and leads down to the woods again. Follow the track down, reversing the route you came up, until you come in sight of a small stone house on the right of the brook. Take the path towards it. It leads into a lane that goes past a small reservoir and overlooks a mill. Turn left at the first houses you come to and very quickly you will be on the road to the mill where you started.

Musbury Tor from High Hollinbank

THE ASCENT OF MUSBURY TOR   WALK NO. **3.5**

Musbury Tor is a steep sided, flat topped hill only 1114 ft. (338 metres) high. It is fringed with rocks on three sides and looks quite impressive. It is possible to park in the car park of Barlows Mill at week-ends and in the evening. This is quite close by, but on the opposite side of the road to the Higher Mill Museum. See Walk No. 3.6 for further guidance.

Time: about ¾ hour return.

Walk up the old road that leaves on the left of the mill and leads to Higher Hollinbank. At this house go through the swing gate into the yard and across the yard into the field below the wall. Do not go through the gate that seems to lead directly to the Tor. Keep below the wall, and turn left with it when it swings up the hill. Where it meets the next wall you will find a stile, and over this a track slanting up left and climbing quite gently leads to the top. Views over Haslingden and up the Rossendale Valley are very good, and if it is clear, you can see Ingleborough and Penyghent. It's a particularly worthwhile walk late in the evening when all the street lamps are lit and the Valley spread at your feet in a pattern of coloured lights. Return as you came.

TWO WALKS AROUND MUSBURY CLOUGH

Musbury Clough is overlooked by the Tor and is one of the nicest spots on the eastern side of the Recreational Area. It has trees, a little lake, a trout stream and some deep-cut hollows climbing steeply up to the moor. Both walks start at the same place, one is quite short taking only 30-40 min., the other about 1½ hours.

Approach on the B6232 and park at Higher Mill Museum. This now has a public car park. See p23 for details. Turn left along the road and right after about 200 yds onto a cinder track that goes through Barlow's Mill to some cottages and then through a gate on the left. Be careful to shut it and the next one as this is grazing land. Where this track meets a walled lane going sharply left by a row of cottages the shorter walk goes left up the walled lane and the longer one crosses the stream.

For the short walk, retrace you steps to the row of cottages and take the track that runs between walls up to Higher Hollinbank. Here, on the right, there are two gates in a corner. Go through the lower one and follow the wall until it turns up the hill. Then keep straight on, neither climbing nor descending, until the path becomes clear. Then it drops gently to the brook. Cross the brook by a little bridge, climb the wall by the stile, turn right and follow the path back to your car. You can do this walk the other way round but it is probably easier to find the paths this way. It is also possible to climb the Tor whilst you are up at Higher Hollinbank. See Walk No. 3.5 for the details, and allow an extra 30 min.

For the longer walk, go up the wall side by the stream, cross the wall by the stile and turn right. (This is the reverse of the short walk). Climbing up the hill, a little way past a small artificial lake the track makes a sharp turn left to go to three farms, now in ruins. Follow this past the third ruin, there's very little left now, and at the bend in the track just past it, aim at a row of five hawthorn trees which is about two fields away. Just here the track is very faint but at the trees it is better marked. Keep walking in the same direction until you meet a track coming in from the right that encircles the valley head. Turn left on it and follow it round, crossing the three streams that make the valley head. After the third one, climb gently up to the top wall, but do not cross the stile there. It leads to Gt. House Farm. Instead, walk along neither climbing nor descending for a little way until you find a path that leads below the rocks of the Tor. Follow this above the wall until you come to the stile. Go over it, follow the wall turning right when it turns, until it brings you into the lane at Higher Hollinbank. Turn left and 5 min. will see you back to your car.

Things of interest

Musbury Clough was the site of a medieval deer park. It reached up to the the moor, across into the next clough, Alden Clough, and over to where Holden Wood reservoir is situated today. The whole was walled or fenced to keep the deer in, and of course, was heavily wooded. Crumbling stone walls abound in the valley and the untrained eye cannot distinguish the deer park boundaries amongst them. There is good documentary evidence for the boundaries, and for other deer parks within the Area. This deer park was created by the Lords of Clitheroe in 1304 A.D. in order to retain and conserve deer for their hunting pleasures. These pleasures didn't last long for in 1322 A.D. the King confiscated it because of acts of treason by Thomas of Lancaster at the Battle of Borough Bridge. In 1408 A.D. it was no longer a hunting ground and was carved up into lots and sold in 1507 A.D. Two hundred and fifty years later the valley housed a dozen small farms and several woollen mills. The people worked in the mill and kept a few cows and sheep. Then came the various towns seeking catchment areas for water supplies. The little lake you pass on this walk collects Musbury water and sends it through a leat to the Grane Reservoirs. In Spring, mooorland birds, the curlew and lapwing especially, are often seen in the higher parts of the valley. Sometimes there's a carrion crow. In the trees, thrushes, blackbirds and chaffinches abound. Pied wagtails can be seen by the stream.

A VISIT TO THE GREAT HOUSE FARM TRAIL, HELMSHORE

Great House Farm belongs to the Ministry of Agriculture, Fisheries and Food and was acquired by them in 1951. It carries out experimental work in hill farming methods and has recently laid out a farm trail along the lines of a nature trail. Wellies are recommended in wet weather as some parts can be very muddy. It is reported that Great House Farm is to be closed by the Ministry and it is not known what will happen to this walk.

Time: about 1 hour.

The Approaches

If you are travelling from the Blackburn direction, take the B6232 road to Bury, and follow this through Helmshore to the White Horse: if from other directions this is the place to find. Here a side road is sign-posted to the Great House Experimental Farm. Go up this road and then turn right after about 300 yards. The road climbs steeply and then drops down to an old mill and a row of cottages. Turn left in front of the cottages, then still climbing steeply up the hill, keep right, left, and left again into the car park just below the farm buildings. Buy the pamphlet from the slot machine (10p), and you're ready to start.

The Walk

The walk starts by going straight up the farm yard past the building to the top gate where you turn left. Now it is adequately but not generously sign-posted with little white painted arrows. Every point of interest has a board that tells you a bit more about what you can see there, and an elaborate arrow that starts you off again in the right direction. It's the black part of the arrow that you follow. There's a picture of both the farm and the arrow on the front of the pamphlet. Between the 5th and 6th 'check points' you can make an extension up to Township of Pilkington, an elaborate name for one of the many ruined farms in these valleys. If you're thirsty, it's worth a visit for there is a spring and drinking trough of very good water. Keep high in the field to find the stile and return low down to the other stile. There's a ditch to be crossed that needs a good stride, and then it's all pleasant walking back to the car park.

Pendle Hill behind Musbury Tor
and Great House Farm, Helmshore.

A VISIT TO ROBIN HOOD'S WELL, HELMSHORE
WALK NO. **3.8**

The well is on the old moorland road from Helmshore to Bury. Its age is not known, but it seems unlikely it ever had anything to do with Robin Hood. Today the spring that feeds it is still running but has been diverted for agricultural purposes. There is some talk of restoring it.

Park at the White Horse on the B6232. See Walk No. 3.7 for instructions on how to find this pub.

Time: about 50-60 min. return.

Walk up the lane that leads to Gt. House Farm, but keep straight on at the first junction instead of turning right to the farm. Turn left at the next junction and continue to the road end at Dowry Head. Note that it is not possible to park or even pass on the last bit of lane. The old road, steep and muddy, starts here and runs up the hill between walls for about ½ mile. The well is on the right just before you reach the gate. Return as you came.

If you like you can continue up Bull Hill from here. Go through the gate and take the lowest of the tracks and continue along it until you meet Walk No. 3.1 at the point where it passes the wood and the old mine heaps. Time for this extension: about 2 hours.

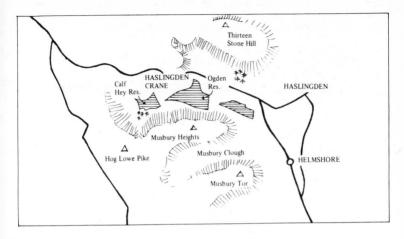

THE ROUND OF MUSBURY HEIGHTS AND HOG
LOWE PIKE   WALK NO. **3.9**

This very fine walk has some hard going and boots are strongly recommended. Views are exceptionally fine and varied if it is done this way round.

Time: about 2½ hours.

Park near the Holden Arms, Haslingden. It is at the junction of the B6231 Blackburn-Haslingden road and the B6235 road. The path starts as a tarmac road next to the pub's car park and goes down to the Holden Wood Reservoir. (Alternative car parking here.) Keep on it until a branch goes off left to Hill End Farm, then go up this muddy lane to the farm. As soon as you're through the gate above the farm, turn right through a gap in the wall and follow sheep tracks slightly downhill towards the fence. Make for a ruined barn and just beyond it you will find a stile in the fence that puts you firmly on a better track. Follow this along the edge of the steep ground until you come to a ramp leading down from Musbury Heights Quarry to Ogden Reservoir. There is a tunnel through the ramp but it is unsafe and it is better to cross the ramp by one of the many sheep tracks. On the other side you will find another stile and better going for a time. The track passes two ruined farms and then tends to split up into a number of faint ones. Keep to your level as near as you can. A ditch with a raised edge is good guidance and leads you to a gap in the trees where you will find yet another ruined farm. Here a pleasantly grassy cart track climbs steeply up through the wood. When you come to a

103

The Ramp, Musbury Heights Quarry

grassy clearing near the top of the trees turn right along it to the fence. Duck under the wire fence and follow the stream up Hog Lowe Clough. This bit is very hard going as there's no path. Where the stream forks take the right hand one and keep your eye open for the appearance of a path on its right hand side. Cross over as soon as you see it and be done with some particularly hard going. You now follow the stream up towards the wall you can see just ahead . Here a small diversion to the right brings you to the top of Hog Lowe Pike. (1255 ft., 383 metres.) Return to the wall at the top of the little 'pass' that leads over to Broadhead and follow the faint path that follows the wire fence, which is the parish boundary, to the first sharp corner in it. Now turn right and follow an even fainter path about 100 yards from the fence until you come to a wall corner on your left.

At this point the enthusiasts for moorland bog trotting can keep straight on following the fence over Whowell Height and Scholes Height to Bull Hill. There's no right of way and no path. At Bull Hill a sharp turn left will put them on to the old track that runs down to Alden Brook where they can pick up the Gt. House Farm Trail paths, go over the back of Musbury Tor to Higher Hollinbank and then down to the road where 15 minutes will see them back to their cars. Allow 4 hours for this extended walk.

But back to that wall corner! Don't go through the hole in the wall, but stay on the left side when an old track will soon be under your feet. It goes through the wall at the next corner and then bends away leftwards and keeps most of its height. The path isn't well trodden, but unmistakably follows the line of one of the old roads that used to lead to the farms. It keeps bending left and eventually ends at a gateway long since built up with stone. Here you have a choice of ways back. If you are short of time, make a fairly sharp right turn down the hill first towards a clump of trees and then towards a wall corner where there is a vertical slot, quite easily seen. Pass this wall corner on the right to a gateway, go through it and dropping a little and keeping right you will find another gateway. Do not follow sheep tracks to the left. After this the track becomes a good deal more distinct. Just before it comes to a ruined building a branch goes uphill to the left. It's beween two walls and is extremely narrow, only wide enough for one person. After 50 yards or so the walls end and the path drops gently down to the next ruin. Go right down to the fence as soon as you can, for this is the path, although the gateway has been built up. Hill End Farm is now in sight quite close, and from there retrace your steps to your car.

If you are interested in Industrial Archaeology, you may prefer to finish through the Musbury Heights Quarry. The chimney stack is just visible from near the blocked gate where you take you choice of routes. At this point, instead of going right and sharply downhill, go only slightly right and towards a massive wall ahead. It's not the sort you would want to climb, and there's no need to. Drop down a little more and keep going and you will find a blocked gateway with a stile. Over this a path takes you direct to the chimney and the ruins of the engine house. The old ginney waggon track goes off to the right. Follow this, and when you're through the first gate, a 50 yard diversion to the left will bring you to the top of the ramp whose base you crossed at the start of the walk. Then continue down the track to Hill End Farm.

Things of interest
Holden Wood and Calf Hey reservoirs were built by Bury Corporation Water Works around 1897. (See Walk No. 3.10 for more detail.) Hog Lowe Pike is a mound of special interest because it just might be a Bronze Age burial mound like Round Loaf, Anglezarke. Evidence for this lies in its shape, its position on the edge of the moor, and its name, for Lowe is

derived from an Anglo-Saxon word meaning burial place.

There's another archaeological possibility, too. If you do this walk in winter on a fine day and find yourself at the wall corner above the Musbury Valley at about 2 pm, look across the slopes to the right of the Tor. If conditions are right, you will see in three places a pattern of stripes running straight down the hill made by the sun casting shadows of sets of faint parallel ridges of earth not otherwise visible. They are probably the remains of some ancient field system.

Chimneys in quarries are most unusual, but Musbury Height Quarry seems to have been unusual in more ways than that. There is a vast area covered in spoil heaps, now well grown over, but nowhere is there any commensurate quarry face, only a collection of insignificant holes in the ground. However, the chimney is the boldest remaining part of the engine house that evidently powered the haulage of waggons both to the ramp and down at least one incline. If you examine the path as it leaves the chimney you will see the remains of wooden railway sleepers still embedded in it. Further along, through the gate, you can see great paving stones with deep grooves that could only have been worn in them by the passage of the waggons. This path must then have been part of the incline system of the quarry.

Hog Lowe Pike

A WALK ROUND CALF HEY RESERVOIR

WALK NO. **3.10**

See Walk No. 3.11 for guidance and park about ½ mile further up the road, where an unsignposted tarmac lane leaves at a sharp angle. There's just room to park. Suitable for shoes and any weather.

Time: ¾ hour.

Go down this pleasant lane as far as Calf Hey House. Just as the road goes through the gate to the house there is a swinging gate into a narrow walled passage. Go along here and when it emerges onto a sort of cross roads, take the left hand track and go across the dam. It gives very fine views of the reservoir and the surrounding moors. A good track continues right round the reservoir, crosses the inlet stream by a little bridge and climbs up the hill a little whilst swinging right to rejoin the route at the 'cross roads'. Then return as you came.

Things of interest

As you walk down the tarmac lane you come to a derelict house on the right. Just before it is an old grave-yard. There are grave stones dated 1820-1830, and in contrast, a modern one stating that here was the site of the Methodist Chapel of the village of Haslingden Grane, built in 1815 and demolished in

1955. There is another similar grave-yard by the side of the main road, just below the lane where you started. Here a Cross carries a plate inscribed to the effect that this is where the Church of St. Stephen, parish church of Haslingden Grane, used to stand. It was pulled down and re-erected stone by stone on a site 1½ miles nearer Haslingden and reconsecrated in 1927. Haslingden Grane was a thriving moorland village vacated when the Ogden reservoir was completed in the mid-twenties. Calf Hey and Holden Wood are much older, being completed by Bury Corporation Water Works before the turn of the century. Today the North West Water Board administers all of them.

Musbury Tor, Bull Hill and Musbury Heights from the path up Thirteen Stones Hill.

CLIMBING THIRTEEN STONE HILL   WALK NO. **3.11**
This pleasant moorland hump, one of the northern outliers of the Area, can be climbed direct from Haslingden or Oswaldtwistle, or most easily from Heap Clough which is about 1½ miles up the Haslingden-Blackburn road, the B6232, from Haslingden. On the right hand side of the road are two blocks of houses, one traditionally built, one fairly modern. Park on the verge opposite them. The path starts between them and is marked by a finger post.

Time: 35 min to the top, 1 hour for the return trip, and 2½ hours for the extended trip, which is not recommended unless you have boots and there has been a spell of dry weather.

The cart track turns first into some disused quarries. A little distance in, two tracks bear off to the right whilst the main quarry track swings left. Your track is the second on the right. It leads pleasantly to the upper pastures. When you've gone through the gap in the wall turn right, (this track starts in Haslingden). After about 100 yards a faint tractor trail goes off to the left and soon takes you to the top of the hill. There's no cairn. Return as you came unless you want to take the extended walk to Dry Hill and Rushy Hill.

From Thirteen Stone Hill a good expanse of open moorland stretches for a couple of miles to the west. There are no tracks except animal tracks and it can be pretty wet. From the top of Thirteen Stone Hill aim at Dry Hill. After some time you will come to a wide shallow ditch marking the parish boundary and running precisely in the direction you require. Follow it on either bank because this is easier than the moor itself. Make a diversion to Dry Hill if you wish. The ditch runs ever less deeply almost to the top of Rushy Hill. There is an O.S. cairn a little way to the right, and the road over Grane is just in sight. Drop down to the ruined building which lies between you and the road. Here you will find a not very well marked track that runs along the top side of the wall back to the quarry. In places the wall has disappeared but the line to follow is obvious. Keep going until you come to the last ruined farm before the quarry. Turn right here, and you will soon be on one of the disused quarry tracks that you can see, and another few minutes will see you back to your car.

Things of interest
Thirteen Stone Hill takes its name from the stone circle that once stood on its summit. The stones have long since disappeared, no doubt utilised for wall building, and only the sockets remain. These are shallow, roughly circular depressions, saucer-like, 6-10 ft. in diameter and arranged in a circle. They take a bit of seeing, and it requires the eye of faith to see very much there at all. If there happen to be thirteen of you, you could try standing one in each saucer as you find them and gauge the effect. Perhaps best done in mist or on the edge of dark! Local people sometimes watch the Midsummer's Day sunrise from here as it is a very good viewpoint.

If you are botanically minded, it's mostly sedge, not grass, that grows on the top of the hill. There's plenty of heath rush, too, and further along the wide shallow ditch that you follow to Rushy Hill, you will find the hop sedge growing.

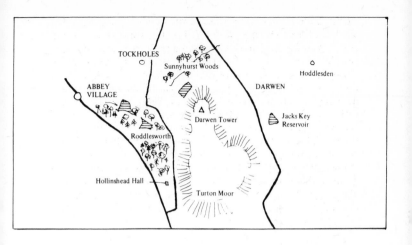

4. WALKS AROUND DARWEN AND TOCKHOLES

More paths have been lost and stiles closed in the pastures to the east and south of Darwen than possibly anywhere else in the Area. Even the paths up Greystone Hill are lost in moorland growth and give walking that is too hard to be worth while, in fact a large chunk of land yields no worthwhile walking.

111

Darwen Tower

WALKING ON THE DARWEN MOORS

WALK NO. **4.1**

Being centrally placed within the West Pennine Moors Area, and having a network of good paths, these moors offer the very epitome of moorland walking — wide horizons, open skies, good going under foot. Two short walks are given, but you can easily link them together for a longer one. Suitable for shoes in good dry conditions.

1. Around the Northern End

Time: 1¼-1½ hours.

Start at The Royal Arms Hotel, Tockholes. This is on the minor road that leaves the A6062 at Ewood, Blackburn, and runs through Tockholes to join the A675 half way between Belmont and Abbey Village. You'll find room to park near the hotel. There are also buses from Darwen and Blackburn.

Go through a gate at the right hand side of a row of stone

112

cottages called Hollinshead Terrace. A wide gravel track crosses the fields and then enters a wooded valley. A little way up this it makes a sharp horse-shoe bend to the left, and just after the bend, you leave this track for another one going quite steeply up on the right. Follow it for a little way, then leave it sharply on the left, climbing even more steeply up to the path that runs round the top edge of the moor to the Tower. Turn left on this track and follow it to the Tower. Climb the staircase within the Tower and enjoy the shelter of the 'greenhouse' on the top if it's windy. There's a grand view from it. (See Walk No. 4.2 for a note of what you can see.) The track now runs round the edge of the moor overlooking Darwen. Follow it round and down a wide hollow and take the second path to the right. This one runs back over the highest point of the moor to Lyon's Den, a ruined farmhouse at the head of the little valley where you started. The path that you are following is joined by others that criss-cross the moor, but keep aiming at the head of the valley where the path curves gently into it. Now follow the track down the valley to the horse-shoe bend where you will re-join the path where you started.

Another starting point, giving a longer walk, is the Sunn-hurst Inn Darwen. See Walk No. 4.12 for details on how to find it and get to Darwen Tower from it. Then follow the above walk until you meet a good path coming in on you right at a sharp angle. Turn right on it and almost at once you will find another one going off left that runs around the edge of the moor and will bring you back to the Tower. Time for this walk: about 2 hours.

2. The Central part

Time: 1¼-1½ hours.
Park at the end of the minor road mentioned above just before it joins the A675. There is plenty of room.

Walk along this road to its first sharp corner. There you will find a stile leading to a grass track. After about 200 yards take the left hand branch. It climbs gently past a ruined farm to a wall on the top of the moor. Don't go astray on a left hand branch. At the top by the wall is an old seat with a fine view and a finger post indicating the way to Belmont, Darwen and Turton. Take the path to Darwen. It passes two old minework-ings and crosses over to the Darwen side of the moor. As it starts to drop down and swing to the right, you will see another track coming up from Darwen, one that goes back over the moor to Lyon's Den. Take this track, keep left at the next junction, and keep on until you reach Lyon's Den. Here, instead of turning down the valley, take the track that crosses an old bridge and then climb up to the skyline. Go through the fence and drop down to the road by the wide grass track. Turn left on the road and 15 minutes of gentle downhill walking will return you to your car.

3. The combined walk
Time: about 2½ hours.

If you want to make a real afternoon of it over these moors, start and finish by the second of the two walks described above. When you have passed the old pits and have reached the track coming up from Darwen, turn right on it and drop down a little into the valley until you can see a small track by a wall on the left climbing up on to the edge of the moor again. Follow this until you come to the Tower. This bit of track gives fine views over Darwen including a 'close up' view of the elaborate chimney at India Mill. From the Tower follow the track along the northern and western edges of the moor. Where the path forks above the little valley, take the left hand branch following a fence. Cross the next path that comes in from the left and continue slightly rightward. The path then goes through the fence and down slightly to Lyon's Den at the head of the little valley. There you rejoin the second route. Definitely the best walk on the Darwen moors.

Things of interest
Most people associate freedom of access to the moors with Derbyshire: few know that they owe their freedom to walk the Darwen Moors to the public spirited action of a few Darwen men led by Mr. W. T. Ashton. The struggle began in 1878, when many of the rights of way established during the heyday of the coal mining industry on the moors were becoming blocked and paths destroyed by the owners of the sporting rights. Mr. Ashton, who had a good knowledge of the rights of way, organised what became a long drawn out legal battle, and on his death in 1894, his sons purchased the shooting rights of Darwen Moor Common and vested them in the Corporation. On the death of the Lord of the Manor free access to the rest of the moor was also vested in the Corporation. On Sept. 6th 1896 a large procession went over the moor to the spot where the Tower now stands to celebrate the freedom of the moors. (See Walk No. 4.2 for a note about the Tower.)

As just noted many of the good tracks that cross the moor were made for access to the old coal pits whose spoil heaps are dotted around. The shafts of these pits were originally lined with stone, but most of them have crumbled and weathered to a cone shaped hollow. Some are full of water, others of earth. The first one that you pass on the second walk (above) has its stone lining in good condition and is worth a cautious look. The lining seems to reach down for 25 or 30 ft, until it reaches good solid rock. If you toss a stone down, it goes a long way in several bounces before it stops. These old shafts were about 200 ft deep — quite shallow by modern mining standards. They worked the Upper Mountain Seam, which varied from 24 to 42 inches thick. The Lower Mountain Seam outcrops in Stepback Brook where the first walk starts and was once mined there.

Hollinshead Terrace at Tockholes was built as a row of mill cottages by Eccles Shorrock, a Darwen cotton manufacturer, for the workers at his nearby factory, now demolished and vanished. This same man also built India Mill whose campanile-like chimney can be seen so well from the moors. It was built in 1867, is 300 ft. high, and its huge foundation stone was quarried at Cadshaw. (See Walk 2.2).

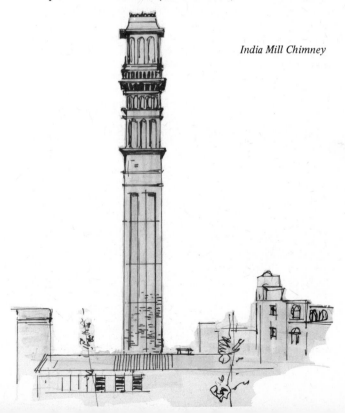

India Mill Chimney

SUNNYHURST WOODS AND DARWEN TOWER
WALK NO. **4.2**

Where else in the Area is there a walk leading to the moors that starts within 100 yards of the main road in the centre of a town and goes right to the top only crossing a tarmac road once? Time: 1 hour, 1 hr. 40 min. return.

Approaching from Blackburn along the A666, about a mile after crossing the borough boundary, you will see the Co-operative stores on the right. The main entrance to the Woods is at the end of Falcon Avenue, which is the street on its right, but it is better to turn right into Earnsdale St. which is next to St. Cuthbert's Church. Park behind the church and cut through a side street to Falcon Avenue: the entrance to the Woods is just 50 yards away.

Walk up the main pathway in the wooded valley, past the two houses, then take the first left-hand branch of the path, near a curious roofed structure, possibly at one time a bandstand. The path climbs steeply upwards and comes out on the road through a pleasing lichgate, Potter's Gate. Turn left, and opposite the Sunnyhurst Inn, 50 yards further on, a rough lane goes off to the right. Follow this past an old quarry, through a gate up on to the moor. Where the track branches, take the right hand one. Almost immediately you can see the Tower, and you will reach it in another 5 minutes. The views to the north and east are the best in the whole Area. You can almost always see the great hump of Pendle and the long ridge of Longridge Fell close at hand, with the Bowlands behind Longridge. Often you will see Blackpool Tower and Black Combe, the most westerly of the Lakeland Hills. More rarely, if you look up the Ribble Valley you can see Ingleborough with Whernside on its immediate left. Penyghent is much further to the right and is not so easily picked out. You can see Holcombe Hill with Peel's monument to the south-east, but views in that direction are not particularly good.

Instead of returning by the same route, you can extend the walk by returning the full length of Sunnyhurst Woods. Allow an extra 20-30 minutes. Return as far as the old quarry, then turn left through a gateway into a narrow walled lane that crosses the field to a new concrete road. Turn right on this, then left where it joins a cart track 50 yards further on. This track goes to the dam on the Earnsdale Reservoir. Follow it to the last iron gate, where on the right you will see a stile leading to the top end of Sunnyhurst Woods. Follow whichever selection of paths you like. All downhill paths lead to the road.

116

If, on the other hand, you haven't much time for a visit to the Tower drive up the road by the church. At the top of the hill the road swings left and the Sunnyhurst Inn is on the right. It is possible to park at the roadside, and you can pick up the route just described at that point.

Things of interest.
Sunnyhurst Woods are really a corporation park, with the usual network of neat paths and bridges over the stream. The woods were acquired by Darwen Corporation in 1902 to celebrate the coronation of King Edward VII. In common with most town woodlands in this district, they are mainly sycamore, beech, oak, hawthorn and rhododendron. Marsh marigolds and bluebells abound in the Spring, and in one place there is a colony of golden saxifrage, an inconspicuous and relatively rare plant. Higher up the woods bilberry and heather grow in patches, and these plants, together with mat grass, dominate the moorland vegetation. The Tower itself was built in 1897 by the Corporation to mark Queen Victoria's Diamond Jubilee. They seemed rather good at those things then. As so often happens the Tower was later neglected and fell into disrepair. It was restored by public subscription in 1972.

This walk describes a circular tour starting at Sunnyhurst Woods and returning over the local Winter Hill. Alternatively you can return on the bus to either Darwen or Blackburn.

Time: about 2 hours, possibly more depending on the variation you take.

Start the walk through Sunnyhurst Woods exactly as described in Walk No. 4.2. When you come to the bandstand keep straight on instead of bearing left at that point. After that, keep right whenever there is a choice of path — there's plenty and it doesn't matter much which you take as they all come out at the Earnsdale Reservoir dam. Cross the dam if you've come out at the right-hand side and follow the cart track until it joins another at a sharp angle. Turn right here and leave this second cart track after about 100 yards by a pleasant footpath that drops down to the reservoir level and then climbs steadily up through the fields by a clear path and line of stiles to Ryal Fold. Then straight ahead along the lane you will find the road, the Royal Arms Hotel, and the bus stop.

If you want to look round Tockholes you now have to do about 15 min. down the road to a lane labelled Higher Hill Farm and you then reverse the route to the Rock Inn as described in Walk No. 4.5.

There's a shorter but less pleasant way from the Earnsdale Dam. From its right-hand end follow a rough water-worn lane that climbs steeply upwards to a junction. Here take the left hand fork and it will bring you onto the road not far above the lane down to Higher Hill Farm. If you prefer to walk back to Darwen and save your brass, then continue on the road 100 yards past the Rock Inn to a garage on the opposite side of the road. An old bridleway starts there that will bring you back to the Hawkshaw district of Darwen. Take the right hand fork in the clump of trees behind the first farm, and the left one at the second junction. From Heights Farm it's straight down to Darwen.

Things of interest

See Walk No. 4.2 for the notes on Sunnyhurst Woods and Walk No. 4.15 for the notes about Tockholes. Ryal Fold is a group of old farm houses, one of which has been very pleasingly restored. If you do the walk in late June before the hay has been cut, you will see they don't grow grass round Tockholes, just flowers!

Red Lees Farm, Tockholes

FROM ABBEY VILLAGE TO TOCKHOLES
WALK NO. **4.4**

This is a splendid circular walk that passes three of the most picturesque old farms in the Area, and takes you through flower-filled fields and woodland.

Time: about 1 hour.

Abbey Village lies on the A675 Preston-Bolton road close to the old Blackburn-Chorley railway line. Park at the Hare and Hounds, which is opposite the junction with the lane to Brinscall. The Chorley-Blackburn bus stops here.

The walk starts on a cart track by the side of the pub. When you reach the third small clump of trees on the left, look out for a faint footpath going across the field to the right. Follow it through the next stile and straight down the steep hillside to the private road in the valley below. If you miss the short-cut field path, don't worry, the cart track you're on takes the long way round and continues right round to Red Lees Farm. Alternatively you can go across the wooden footbridge when you will climb very steeply into the farm yard.

Red Lees Farm is one of the oldest in the Area with a datestone of 1674 and has been carefully restored. If you have come up the farm road turn right into a lane as soon as you are through the farm gate, but you'll miss the front of the house unless you pop round to the left. If you come by the footbridge, you will be facing it.

Follow this grassy lane (muddy in wet weather), and when you have passed the first bend, look up to the fence on the left to spot the stile by the gate; it's easier to see from here. Only cross over to it when you're at the end of the lane, as the field is often cultivated hay. The path through the pasture is faint, but the stile at the end is into a grassy lane. This takes you past Lower Hill, in some ways even more attractive than Red Lees, and onto a bit of tarmac road at Victoria Terrace. Turn right here up a wide grassy lane to Higher Hill. Turn right immediately you have passed Rose Cottage, and about 50 yards down the lane turn left into a pasture. The stile has a whitewashed reminder, "Keep your dog on a lead." First, however, go ahead a little in order to have a better look at Higher Hill Farm, yet another of these fine old farms. Back to the stile. The path is faint, but go diagonally right to the next stile and then straight down the hill to a white gate that leads you into the woods. Follow the woodland path down to the iron bridge that takes you across the spillway between the Upper and Lower Roddlesworth Reservoirs. Turn right when you come to the embankment and right again into the wood at the end of it. Follow this track to the farm, where, surprise, surprise, the gate across this track is locked. Saved again! There's a stile in the corner by the barn and the wall. This brings you into the farm yard from where a cart track leads to the main road. 10 minutes along it will see you back to your car. There's a footpath, and the road banking is thick with flowers in summertime.

Things of interest
See Walk No. 4.5 for notes about Tockholes. If you turn left where you join the road at Victoria Terrace you can wander along to have a look at St. Stephen's Church. Add about 30 minutes to the time if you do this. The two Roddlesworth reservoirs and the lower Rake Brook Reservoir were built by Liverpool Corporation at about the same time as the Anglezarke and Rivington Reservoirs. Water from the Roddlesworth Reservoirs flows into the Anglezarke Reservoir through the Goit, best seen at White Coppice. (See Walk 1.10).

Tockholes School

A LOOK AROUND TOCKHOLES   WALK NO. **4.5**

Tockholes, pronounced 'Tockles' for the benefit of the unin-
itiated, isn't just a village like Belmont or Turton, nor is it a
suburb of Blackburn. It's a rural area of considerable charm
nestling on the western slopes of Winter Hill, not *the* Winter
Hill, but another one in the north-west corner of the Area. It
isn't even on a road to anywhere in particular, and some of the
most interesting buildings lie on a loop road below the minor
road on which the biggest cluster of houses and shops stand.

To find this charming corner by road, get onto the minor
road that runs from the Brown Cow on Livesey Branch Road,
Ewood, Blackburn, to the Preston-Belmont road (A675).
From Blackburn continue up the hill until you reach the Rock
Inn. It's best to park there and then explore the loop road on
foot as this is extremely narrow, and parking, except by St.
Stephen's Church, is almost impossible. Besides, it's a lovely
walk along lanes heavy with the scent of hawthorn, elder flower
and haymaking on a good summer's day. Allow an hour for it.
There are buses from Darwen and Blackburn, or you could
walk all the way from Darwen — see Walk No. 4.3.

The Rock Inn itself, though of modern appearance, has a
datestone for the year 1791. Turn down the lane besides the
Inn and continue steeply down the hill to the vicarage and
church. The vicarage wall has built into it an old stone archway
dated 1692, and a little lower down a double Norman arch

121

spans a well, built into the wall. A worn, almost illegible inscription at the back tells you that this archway was brought from Garstang Hall when it was demolished in 1903 and re-erected by the vicar of that time. Unfortunately the pipe that feeds the well no longer runs. Pass on, entering the church yard by the lichgate. On the right you will see Tockholes' first school built in 1854, and now being restored.

Its most interesting feature is an external pulpit. You can imagine the crowds seated on the grass beneath the trees when congregations were bigger than today. Go on to the Church of St. Stephen, a very pleasing modern structure incorporating a fragment from an earlier building. There has been a series of churches on this site dating from 884 A.D. Of similar antiquity is the Toches Stone which stands on the left just before you reach the church. The base on which the stone stands bears the following explanatory inscription:

"The upper portion of this monument is supposed to be a remnant of the old parish preaching cross, probably dating to 884 A.D. The lower portion is probably a part of the ancient Toches Stone from which the parish takes its name."

There is an interesting reminder of the Industrial Revolution in this church yard — John Balderston's grave. It lies behind the church on the right and states simply:

John Balderston
Inventor of the weft fork
Born 1780   Died 1862

Like many inventors, Balderston made no money out of his invention and died a pauper. Though not of such outstanding importance as Crompton's spinning mule, cotton manu-facturers of the time made plenty of money out of it, and erected this memorial some time after his death.

Now leave the church yard and continue along the lane. In a few hundred yards you will come to another church, Tockholes United Reformed Church, founded in 1662, re-built in 1710 and again in 1880. Non-conformism has always been strong in the moorland villages, nowhere more than here. On Black Bartholomew's Day 1662, the people of Tockholes refused to adopt the Prayer Book under the Act of Uniformity and left the Church to establish their own form of worship. So too, did the people of Rivington.

Continue a little further along the lane and there, on the right is yet another Church, the Bethesda Mortuary Chapel, fittingly with its own graveyard. No wonder the whole district is known as Chapels! Spare a glance for the row of cottages on your left, and if you have time, turn right for a diversion to Lower Hill Farm, a fine old manor house and a Grade 2 listed building. Then keep straight on up the footpath. It's an ordinary footpath between wide walls, but most curiously, has a pair of regulation Ministry of Transport signs saying, 'No road for motor vehicles except for access'. They'd have a job! The footpath turns sharp left behind the row of cottages on your left at the top of the hill, and takes you back to the centre of the village opposite the Victoria, but before doing that, go just a little further up the lane and look to your right to see Higher Hill Farm. It's another fine old farm house whose main claim to fame is its 'lofty loo', still to be seen jutting out into fresh air on the first floor of the east wall. It must have been a great convenience in the days of primitive sanitation.

Back to the Victoria, then, a mock Tudor affair with black wooden beams bolted on to a solid stone building just for effect. Still, it's not unpleasing. Here you are back to the road on which the Rock Inn stands. Turn left, and less than 10 minutes will see you there.

Lower Hill Farm, Tockholes

THE RODDLESWORTH NATURE TRAIL, TOCKHOLES

This walk starts almost opposite the Royal Arms Hotel, Tock-holes, where you can buy a pamphlet describing it. It will take you about an hour just to do the walk, more if you start hunting for and identifying plants. Whether or not this is your particular interest, this walk is quite the finest and longest woodland and stream-side walk in the whole Area.

To find the Royal Arms Hotel, get on to the minor road that runs from Ewood, Blackburn to join the A675 Preston-Bolton road near Belmont. From Blackburn the road climbs steadily and you pass three more pubs, until, almost below Darwen Tower, you will find the Royal Arms. There is room to park at the side and if the day is good, a superb view, almost as good as that from Darwen Tower, and without effort.

The Nature Trail Committee has done a great deal of work to improve the path with gravel and steps and it is suitable for shoes and any weather. It is worth noting that the return from the river is long and steep — elderly people will find it easier to do the walk the other way round. There is a map at the start and you need little guidance to follow the way. Just remember to follow the riverside path at the bridge or you'll end up in Abbey Village, a couple of miles away.

Things of interest
The pamphlet goes into this very thoroughly. The only criticism to be made is that at the time of writing, Spring 1977, the various numbered stations mentioned in the pamphlet are no longer easily visible, which makes location of plants and features much more difficult. No doubt the Committee will remedy this. In any case, it is a superb walk.

A VISIT TO THE WISHING WELL OF HOLLINSHEAD HALL

The well lies east of the Bolton-Preston road A675, two miles south of Abbey Village. It is not marked on the map and you approach by a footpath starting about 100 yards south of a farm called, strangely, Piccadilly. This is the first building on the east side of the road if you are travelling south from Abbey Village. You can just park on the verge, but you need to be careful, it is a fast road.

Time: 30-40 min. for the return trip.

Go through the swing gate and follow the path through the trees for about ten minutes. The path becomes indistinct, but by then you will be able to see the Well House as a small barn-like building on the right. Go into the Well House. It's a bit dark, but you will soon see water pouring from the mouth of a stone lion into a deep trough and then into two deep recesses on either side of the lion. It is quite impressive and a little bit eerie.

The date of the building is not known, though the style may be described as rural Georgian. It may have been built when the nearby Hollinshead Hall, now utterly ruined and vanished, was rebuilt in 1776. The building was restored by Liverpool Corporation in 1905, presumably at about the time the Roddlesworth reservoirs were built. The well was known in medieval times and reputed to have curative properties for eye troubles. In fact, the water is diverted from a tiny stream nearby into a sort of tank behind the building and then to the lion. The Well House is now a listed building.

You may also visit the Wishing Well by making a long extension to the Roddlesworth nature trail. This will take about 2 hours.

A VISIT TO JACK KEY'S RESERVOIR, DARWEN
WALK NO. 4.8

This pleasant spot lies on the south side of Darwen just off the main A666 road to Bolton, not far from the cemetery. It is right on the edge of the map, sheet S D 72. Accrington.

The path to it starts from the end of Knowsley Road which is most easily found by looking for the minor road to Hoddlesden which is prominently sign-posted. Knowsley Road is the next one up the hill. There's a bus stop there too.

Park at the end of Knowsley Road by the houses. The road continues past a school and becomes a cinder track leading up to a gate that opens onto the reservoir bank. A good track goes along the embankment and the far bank. A left turn there will take you up the fields to Cranberry Fold, from where a pleasant lane leads you back to Darwen, or it is possible, though not very salubrious because of the closeness of the Corporation rubbish tip, to cross the inlet stream by a little bridge and walk right round. The paths are poor. Nevertheless, with its grassy shores and good views of Darwen Tower and Moors, Jack Key's Reservoir is a pleasant spot for an evening stroll, especially if the wind is in the north!

Rivington Pike

5. THE THREE TOWERS OF LANCASHIRE

This is the great classic walk of the Area, taking in the towers of Rivington, Darwen, and Holcombe. It is usually done from Georges Lane, Horwich, to Holcombe and will take 6½-7½ hours. Many variations are possible, but the route described here does not look for difficulties and uses a fair number of paths not otherwise covered in this book. It is best to park in Bolton and to use public transport for the start and finish, though unfortunately this virtually rules out Sundays.

Take the bus from Moor Lane bus station, Bolton, to Georges Lane, Horwich, and follow that lane right to the Pike. 30-40 minutes is sufficient to see you there, a useful boost to morale! Return to the rough moorland road that Georges Lane has become and follow it to its junction with the Belmont-

Rivington road. (A more sporting walk takes in Winter Hill. Passing the T.V. masts, turn left to the Post Office mast and keeping left until the O.S. cairn is seen on the right. Then drop down to the road, rejoining the main route.)

Just over the crest of the road you will see a gate on the left. A wettish track runs down towards Belmont from it. Cross the wall at the deserted farm and continue to Belmont by a cinder track.

Turn left when you reach the main road. In about 2-3 hundred yards a short-cut footpath leads down to the road that crosses the dam. As soon as you are across the dam take the farm road that leads to Lower and Higher Pasture Houses. As you go through the farm the track tends to the right a bit and then joins a cart track. Turn left on this and follow it until it reaches the road. Keep on this road for a good half mile until you see a broad grassy track on the right. It is sign-posted 'Footpath to Lyon's Den'. Follow this track up the side of Cartridge Hill and go through a stile in the wall on the top of the ridge.

You can now see Darwen Tower quite clearly, but it doesn't pay to make a bee line for it. Keep to the track you are on, cross the old stone bridge and keep straight ahead, climbing just a little. After about 5 minutes there is a three way junction of tracks. You want the left hand one which runs parallel to the valley on your left, whilst dropping down slightly. Go straight ahead at the next 'cross roads', still bearing left a little, until you meet the track that climbs up the valley and contours the edge of the moor on the north side and leads to the Tower. This is Tower No. 2 safely in the bag. Now comes the hard part! Turn south and follow the good track that runs round the edge of the moor overlooking Darwen until it drops down into a steep-sided valley. Then turn right on the cart track that comes up this valley, cross the brook and follow the track right round the curve of the moor until it starts to go leftwards. Here you leave it, and it is most important to find the right place or you will have much trouble finding the way over to Cadshaw. There are three tracks, all faint, crossing the moor in various places, and yours is the last one. There is a row of three farms below you as you come along after crossing the brook. The last one has a conspicuous orange roof. Go well past this until you meet a fence coming right down across the track you're on, except for a gap for walkers. Go through this gap, turn right, and follow the line of the fence.

The going is pretty rough, but it improves. Cross the next

fence — there's no stile — and turn left at the next one. The fence becomes a wall. Follow this to a properly constructed sheep gap on the right, just before a tree. Through the gap bear left and follow a rushy hollow until you meet a cart track coming in from the left. Follow this through several fields until it turns right and heads down the valley. Don't follow it down, however. Instead keep straight on below the fence until you can see the big track in the valley below you. Drop down to this and follow it to the road.

Turn left on the road and go up the hill for about 200 yards to where a wide cart track labelled 'Public Footpath' leaves on the right. It runs between walls right down to the Turton and Entwistle Reservoir. About a mile along it take the right hand fork. Shortly after arriving at the reservoir side, you leave it again by a narrow track that runs through the trees and over a field to join the lane that goes down to Entwistle station. Go past the station and across the dam and up to the Edgworth road.

In Edgworth go across the cross-roads and turn left down a cart track by the side of the Rose and Crown. It apparently ends at the first farm cottage, but in fact goes through the white gate, bears left and comes out on the last bit of tarmac road met on this walk. Turn right and keep straight on along a track after the tarmac ends in a couple of hundred yards. This track will bring you to Redearth Farm and the continuation, at present disturbed because of farm reconstruction work, lies straight ahead on the left of the farm. The path bends right over the moor, goes through swing gates and joins the cart track that leads from Hawkshaw to Grainings Farm. Follow the cart track to the T junction, and there keep straight ahead to Holcombe Hey Fold. Go through the farm and follow the faint track that contours the base of the steep ground. Cut across to the ruins of Holcombe Head Farm and climb up the hill very steeply and without track at first, aiming just to the right of Harcles Hill. You will find the track when you cross under the power lines, if not before. Then follow it across the moor and round to the monument. There! You've done it! Tower No. 3 is in the bag.

All that remains is to get down to Holcombe Brook for public transport. Continue along in the direction in which you have been walking, past the farm, and down the zig-zags. There are many confusing tracks here. Aim at Hill End or Hey House and then at the Aitken Sanitorium. Turn right here in order to stay on the bridle-track which will fetch you out by the road junction and bus stop in Holcombe Brook.